'Every salesperson, from new hires to seasoned pros[...] book. *How To Sell* clearly explains the foundational [...] knowledge and practical actions that lead directly to sales success and help you earn more.'

Jeb Blount,
CEO of Sales Gravy and author of *Fanatical Prospecting*

'Finally a book that gets it – sales is about helping, not selling. If you want to transform your conversations with buyers, this is your book.'

Keenan,
author of *GAP Selling*

'Every so often there's a book that truly changes how people think, and *How to Sell* is one of them. Regardless of where you're at in sales you must read this book. *How to Sell* is the North Star for all of us in the sales community. Use this book as your tool to self-correct your direction. Few books will have the impact on your career that this book will.'

Mark Hunter,
'The Sales Hunter' and author of *A Mind for Sales*

'There are so many great ideas and strategies in this book. Pick it up and have a highlighter ready!'

Colleen Stanley,
author of *Emotional Intelligence for Sales Success*

'*How to Sell* is exactly what the sales profession needs right now. This book thoughtfully blends the practical skills you need with the mindset to sell effectively. Steve breaks down complex sales concepts clearly, so they're easy to apply whether you're brand new to sales or a seasoned sales leader. For anyone aiming to improve their sales approach and build lasting customer relationships, this book is a must-read. It will not just help you sell better but also make sales more enjoyable and fulfilling.'

Leslie Venetz,
Founder of The Sales-Led GTM Agency

'I've known Steve for five years and have seen his passion up close, especially when it comes to helping people get into sales and make it a career. I learned sales the hard way. I wish I had this when I started my first sales job. It's clear, practical and tells you exactly what works without the abstract theory. Reading it sharpened me up – and I've been in the sales world for 20 years! If you're serious about getting clients or building a real business, this book will help you do it well and do it right.'

Dean Seddon,
CEO of Maverrik and author of *Get Growing*

HOW TO SELL

EVERYTHING YOU NEED TO THINK, KNOW & DO TO HAVE GREATER SALES CONVERSATIONS

STEVE RADFORD

First published in Great Britain by Practical Inspiration Publishing, 2025

The moral rights of the author have been asserted.

ISBN 978-1-78860-865-7 (paperback)
      978-1-78860-864-0 (hardback)
      978-1-78860-866-4 (ebook)

EU GPSR representative: LOGOS EUROPE, 9 rue Nicolas Poussin, LA ROCHELLE 17000, France Contact@logoseurope.eu

Want to bulk-buy copies of this book for your team and colleagues? We can customize the content and co-brand *How to Sell* to suit your business's needs.

Please email info@practicalinspiration.com for more details.

Practical Inspiration
Publishing

Contents

Dedication

This book is dedicated to all the salespeople I've had the pleasure to teach, coach and mentor. Learning for you, with you and from you has been a deeply satisfying and rewarding experience. Thank you. This book wouldn't have happened without you.

Foreword

In my decades of working with sales professionals across many industries, I've observed a persistent gap in sales literature. While countless books offer advanced techniques for complex sales or focus on specific aspects of selling, very few provide a comprehensive foundation that addresses the mindsets, knowledge and practical skills needed for effective selling across contexts.

How to Sell fills this critical gap magnificently.

As Chairman of the Institute of Sales Professionals, I've dedicated my career to elevating the standards and recognition of sales as a profession. This mission requires resources that teach techniques and instil the ethical principles and customer-focused mindsets that underpin sustainable sales success. This book embodies these values perfectly.

What distinguishes this work is its holistic approach. Rather than simply prescribing what to do, Steve explains why specific approaches work, grounding his recommendations in psychology, neuroscience and behavioural economics. This balance of theory and practice empowers readers to adapt principles intelligently to their unique contexts rather than rigidly following scripts.

The book's three-part structure – How you need to think, What you need to know, and What you need to do – provides a logical progression that builds systematically. The New 7-Step Sale process, with its innovative additions of the 'understand' and 'trial close' steps, represents a significant contribution to sales methodology that aligns perfectly with today's buyer expectations.

Perhaps most importantly, Steve places ethical selling and win-win outcomes at the centre of his approach. By defining selling as 'helping customers to make informed buying decisions by exploring and targeting win-win outcomes', he presents a framework that builds sustainable business relationships while delivering results. This philosophy resonates deeply with the Institute of Sales Professionals' commitment to ethical selling.

Whether you're new to sales and seeking strong foundations, an experienced professional looking to refine your approach, or a sales leader responsible for developing your team, this book offers invaluable insights and practical guidance. The principles Steve shares will help you close more sales and build the trust and relationships that lead to long-term success.

On behalf of the Institute of Sales Professionals, I'm proud to endorse *How to Sell* as an essential resource for anyone committed to sales excellence.

Andy Hough
Founder, Institute of Sales Professionals

Introduction

I've spent over 20 years working with thousands of salespeople across hundreds of businesses, from small companies and individual salespeople, through to large multi-national organizations with teams that span the globe. Despite their differences they all have one thing in common – they all want to be better at selling.

Some have good days or good salespeople who consistently hit their targets, but they often don't know why or, if they do, they struggle to replicate that success. In the worst cases they have salespeople who hate selling.

I get it. Because once upon a time that was me.

Back in the late 1990s I hated sales. At best, I saw salespeople as becoming increasingly irrelevant. At worst, I saw them as pushy, manipulative and unethical. I saw selling as a transaction, not an experience – or certainly not a nice one.

One realization changed that completely – I realized that sales is about helping people. That one shift in thinking transformed my entire approach. I became a better and more successful salesperson and, most importantly, I started to love selling.

Some of you, too, might already believe that sales is about helping. But if it were obvious to everyone, sales wouldn't have such a bad reputation, and far fewer salespeople would struggle with confidence, consistency and closing deals.

I didn't fully grasp this until I stopped focusing on customers and started focusing on salespeople. Running an agency that recruited and managed sales teams for major brands, I found myself developing training to help our teams improve. It was the realization that I love helping salespeople to solve their problems through engaging and effective interactions that led me to truly understand that's what great salespeople do.

That realization supercharged my passion for sales training and led me to dive deep into sales psychology, communication techniques and learning design. I even went back to university to study workplace learning, later developing the UK's first university-level sales qualification. Since then, I've worked on national sales standards, training programmes and professional development initiatives. Through all that experience, three key lessons stand out.

1. **Sales environments constantly shift, but the best salespeople always nail the fundamentals.** They might lay new tools and techniques on top, but the foundations never change – and in today's world they matter more than ever.

2. **Knowing why something works is just as important as knowing how to do it.** Sales isn't about scripts or rigid techniques – it's about adapting to real people in real situations. The best salespeople understand the principles behind what they do, which makes them flexible, authentic and effective.

3. **Salespeople don't have time for fluff.** Any learning needs to be quick to access, easy to understand and immediately useful.

That's exactly what this book is designed to deliver. I'll break down the fundamental mindsets, knowledge and skills that drive real sales results, explaining not just what to do, but why it works, so you can make each technique your own.

At the end of the day, selling is about helping. I love to learn and share what I've learnt in order to help others. I want you to love selling so that your customers love to learn and buy from you too. That's why I wrote this book.

Who this book is for

This book is for frontline salespeople who want to improve; and the sales leaders and managers who want to help them.

As a salesperson, this book will help you to:

1. develop a confident and consistent approach to selling;

2. master the art of value-based sales conversations; and

3. deliver greater sales results.

As a sales leader or manager, this book will help you to:

1. evaluate your new and existing salespeople against a consistent framework, so you know where and how to help them;

2. build on your existing armoury of tools and techniques to help you train, mentor and coach your team to deliver greater sales results; and

3. provide a common language and toolkit that enables shared learning and promotes continuous development.

All salespeople will benefit from reading this book, but the concepts within it are particularly suited to short-chain sales – those that can usually be closed through a single or short chain of sales conversations, with a single or short-chain of decision makers.

In contrast, long-chain sales are those that typically can't be closed without going through multiple stages, and often require the blessing or agreement of multiple stakeholders. Formal procurement and tendering processes for large, multi-year contracts are good examples. In these cases, the selling foundations I'll cover in this book are still essential – long-chain sales start by successfully selling the idea of an initial discovery call or exploratory meeting after all. But this book isn't designed to cover everything you need to know or do to successfully navigate a complex contract negotiation.

That aside, outside of those buyer-controlled, long-chain tender processes, this book covers everything you need to think, know and do to successfully navigate your way through any sales conversation, no matter what you're selling or who you're selling to.

What is and isn't in this book

This book is in three parts.

▶ **Part 1** covers how you need to think. I'll show you how to develop the six essential mindsets that should underpin all of your sales activities.

> ▶ In **Part 2** I'll show you what you need to know, including activities to help you build and organize your customer, company, product and competitor knowledge.

> ▶ In **Part 3** I'll cover what you need to do, giving you the seven-step process you need to follow to have greater sales conversations.

To understand why I've structured the book this way, let's break down exactly what it is that drives your sales performance.

Your personal performance drivers

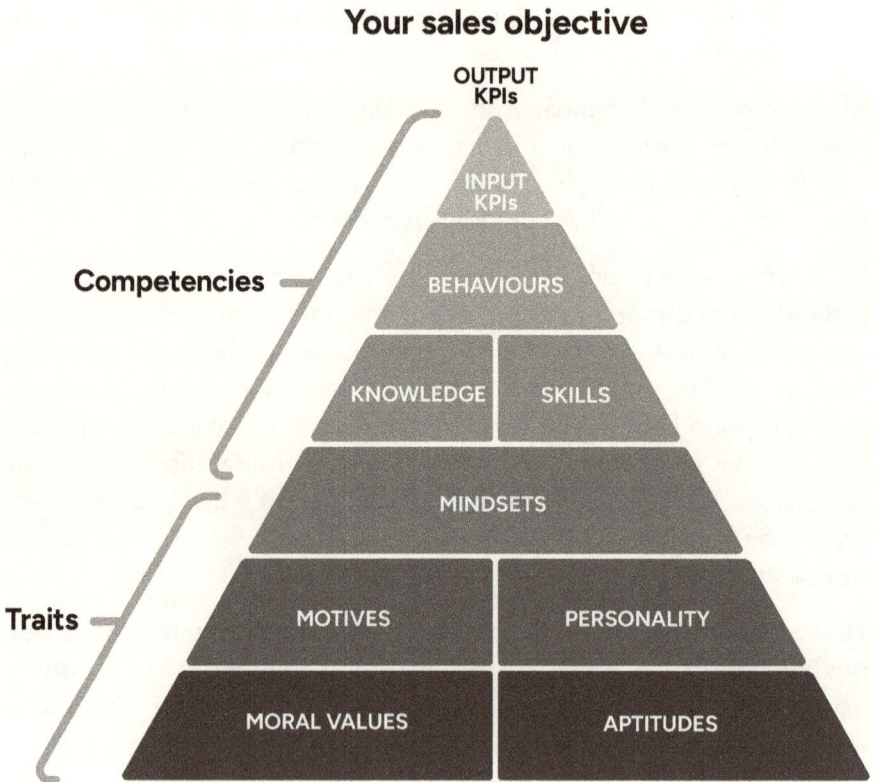

Figure 1: The personal performance drivers pyramid

In Figure 1, the pyramid that points upwards towards your sales target or objective represents you, and all the aspects of you that drive your sales performance. Everything in the lower layers of the pyramid underpins and helps to shape everything in the layers above, all the way up to the behaviours and actions at the top that are directly connected to the sales objective you've been targeted to achieve.

At the base of this pyramid sit your moral values and aptitudes. Your moral values define the things you instinctively believe are right or wrong, whereas your aptitudes define your innate talents and natural abilities – the things you find easy to be good at.

The layer above contains your motives and personality traits. Your motives are what drive you – they're your fundamental reasons for doing things. Your personality traits define who you are or, more accurately, they describe how you'll typically behave in certain situations.

Together, your moral values, aptitudes, motives and personality are your key traits. While they're fundamentally important, what's crucial to understand is that neither you, nor I, can change them. The jury's out on whether they're determined more by nature or nurture, but despite the fact they might change slowly over time, traits are aspects over which we have almost no conscious control.

Because we can't change them, traits are things that an organization needs to focus on at the recruitment stage. Companies need to select people for their traits and develop them for their competencies, because it's competencies that sit above traits in this pyramid.

The layer above your motives and personality contains your mindsets. Your mindsets describe how you tend to think and respond in certain situations and, like any layer in the pyramid, they're affected by everything that sits beneath them. Interestingly, while your mindsets form part of your competencies (because they can be consciously developed), they're also partly trait-like because they can be difficult to change. Changing a mindset is not impossible, but it's easier to shape one than it is to change it completely.

Above your mindsets sits your sales knowledge and skills – what you know and what you can do – then above those sit your sales behaviours, which describe what you actually do and how you do it.

Right at the top of your pyramid sit your key performance indicators or 'KPIs'. These are split into two types: your input KPIs that sit within the pyramid; and your output KPIs that sit just above your pyramid directly below your sales objective.

Your input KPIs are the important sales behaviours that are both measurable and within your direct control, which is why they sit *inside* your pyramid. Your output KPIs are the things that happen as a result of your inputs but are outside of your direct control, which is why they sit *outside* of your pyramid. For example, an input KPI might be the number of calls you make, whereas an output KPI might be the number of sales you successfully close. You can control the number of calls you make, but even the best salesperson can't fully control the number of sales they achieve as a result.

Your focus: mindsets, knowledge and skills

If you exclude the traits you can seek to understand but can't control, the biggest impact you can have on your sales performance is to develop your mindsets, knowledge and skills – because these are the things that directly drive your sales behaviours and KPIs and, ultimately, improve your ability to achieve your sales objectives and targets.

That's why this book focuses on everything you need to think, know and do.

It covers the 18 essential competencies that all salespeople need to develop. But that's not to say there isn't more you can learn!

The concepts, tools and techniques here will form a great framework you can continue to build on. As well as more in-depth training courses and coaching programmes, I've also developed a suite of additional resources to complement what's in this book. These include videos, graphics, downloadable tools and templates, plus further information. You'll find references to these throughout the coming chapters, but you can download them all for free, along with copies of the images and diagrams from this book, by going to greatersales.com/bookextras.

How to use this book

I've packed almost 30 years of sales experience into this book, and I hope I've done so in a way that's simple to understand and easy to action. This book covers a lot of ground, but you don't have to implement everything at once. In fact, as you'll learn in Chapter 6, the best way to improve is to focus on making lots of small improvements over time, rather than trying to make one giant leap forward.

The first time you read this book I encourage you to read it in the order it's presented. That's because some of the concepts I introduce in later chapters will build on those I introduce earlier in the book. But if you hit a chapter that feels daunting, don't worry. Just identify one thing you *can* put into action to make a positive difference, focus on that, and make a note to come back to the chapter later.

This is why I recommend you approach *How to Sell* as a handbook to return to time and again, because you may find you gain new insights each time you do.

So, build at your own pace and keep coming back as you grow. Then perhaps later, you'll return to the book once more as you help others to develop their sales abilities too.

Meet our salespeople

To help bring the concepts, tools and techniques I'm going to share with you to life, throughout this book you're going to meet salespeople from three different sales teams. These teams are fictitious, as are the products and services they sell, but the challenges they face are real.

Each of these teams is a combination of the many different sales teams I've worked with. I've created them specifically to demonstrate how the mindsets, knowledge and skills I'll cover in this book can be successfully applied to a wide variety of different types of sales conversation. I'm confident you'll see some parallels between these teams and the challenges they face, and your own, and I hope that seeing how they've applied what they've learnt to have greater sales conversations will inspire you to do the same.

The Drinkit sales team

Drinkit is the world's first better-than-alcohol beer. It not only matches the look, taste and smell of a traditional alcoholic beer, but through its unique blend of bioactive hops, it's able to mimic the gentle and calming effect of alcohol without any of the associated risks or unwanted aftereffects. Their tagline is 'Stay present and Drinkit, without getting drunk.'

Drinkit has two sales teams: The Drinkit on-trade team, tasked with getting independent pubs and bars to sell Drinkit on draught for consumers to enjoy on the premises. And the Drinkit off-trade team, tasked with getting independent licensed retailers to sell Drinkit in bottles and cans for consumers to take away and enjoy at home. Both teams are also tasked with helping their on- and off-trade customers to sell more beer by supporting promotional activities and directly engaging with consumers on their customers' premises where appropriate.

However, the Drinkit sales teams are not responsible for selling beer directly to their customers. Drinkit's independent customers, both in the on-trade and off-trade, buy their beer via wholesalers and other drinks suppliers who, in turn, buy their beer from Drinkit's national accounts team. So the financial benefit that the Drinkit sales team deliver is only indirectly received by the Drinkit company itself, via the increased stock their wholesale customers then buy as a result.

Drinkit's sales teams are both field-based, which means they primarily have sales conversations with prospects and customers in-person on the customers' premises, and only use phone calls or emails to support their in-person sales conversations.

The SupportIT sales team

SupportIT provide always-on remote IT support for small businesses. They provide a range of services, but their app sits at the core of everything they do. By installing the app on each of their devices, customers get continual protection from malware, ransomware and phishing attacks, along with real-time encryption and cloud backup of their data. But what makes SupportIT unique is that their customers can access personalized IT support any time they need it.

If customers ever have a problem with their device, from small issues such as being unable to connect to a printer, to more significant problems like important software not running correctly, SupportIT's AI assistant is ready to give advice or even directly make changes to the user's device if necessary. If the AI assistant is unable to resolve the problem, the issue can automatically be escalated to a human support manager who can seamlessly take over, no matter what time of day or night. For problems diagnosed as requiring physical intervention to achieve a resolution, SupportIT partners with a national IT retailer who can provide equipment repairs and replacements where necessary.

The key to their always-on IT support is that SupportIT offers services in the UK, in the USA and in Australia. So as one office closes, another office is already up and running, ready to provide support for customers on any side of the globe.

For their always-on support service, SupportIT charge a one-off onboarding fee for each user, and everything except repairs and replacements is then covered under a monthly subscription.

The SupportIT sales team are responsible for finding and directly approaching new prospective customers, selling the benefits of their service and supporting the customer as they sign up to a minimum 12-month agreement. Once the contract is signed, the customer is then handed over to SupportIT's customer care team, who'll look after them from that point.

The SupportIT sales team is an inside sales team. This means they primarily have sales conversations with prospects and customers via phone, video calls and emails – rarely, if ever, meeting customers in person.

The Widget sales team

The Widget sales team work in a giant department store and are tasked with selling high-value items that customers carefully consider before buying – from TVs to luxury watches. They can also upsell services that go with these items such as extended warranties and pay-over-time finance.

The Widget Store doesn't make any of these items itself, nor does it supply any of the add-on services directly. Everything the Widget Store sells can also be bought from other retailers, sometimes for a lower price.

So what's unique about the Widget sales team is not what they sell, but how they sell it. Because the Widget Store's goal is to give every customer a uniquely good buying experience.

As a result, the Widget sales team aren't your typical shop assistants; they're more like personal advisors, relationship builders and sometimes even lifestyle consultants. They understand that purchases can be emotionally driven by factors such as self-reward, celebration, social signalling or exclusivity. So they focus on understanding the customer's personal values and emotional wants, as well as their more pragmatic needs, and speak to those desires without ever being pushy.

In summary

On the face of it, these are three very different sales teams. The SupportIT inside sales team sell services directly to businesses; the Drinkit field sales teams sell products indirectly to businesses and consumers; and the Widget instore sales team sell products and services directly to consumers.

However, as different as they appear to be, all three teams require the same core sales mindsets, knowledge and skills if they're to deliver truly greater sales. Let's explore what these are.

PART 1
HOW YOU NEED TO THINK: THE SIX ESSENTIAL MINDSETS FOR GREATER SALESPEOPLE

Chapter 1
Is it a win-win?

The win-win mindset

In the introduction to this book I explained that I became a happier and more successful salesperson once I realized that sales is as much about helping customers as it is about hitting targets. This is the heart of the win-win mindset.

In this chapter we're going to dive into that more deeply. We'll explore why it's better all round when you focus on outcomes where everybody wins, and avoid any kind of 'win at all costs' thinking.

Embracing a win-win sales philosophy

You don't often hear the words 'sales' and 'philosophy' together in the same sentence. But when you consider that the dictionary definition of a philosophy is that it's 'a theory or attitude that acts as a guiding principle for behaviour', then it becomes perfectly natural that you *should* have an underlying philosophy that helps to guide your sales activities.

But before we get ahead of ourselves, what about sales? What does the dictionary have to say about the act of selling?

If you look up the verb 'to sell' in the dictionary, you'll find a number of different definitions. You'll find a transactional definition like this one:

Selling: to transfer goods or render services in exchange for money.

Example: 'She sold me a loaf of bread for £3.'

You'll also find a persuasive purchase definition like this one:

Selling: to persuade or induce someone to buy something.

Example: 'She sold me a different model than I'd planned on buying.'

You'll also find a definition which explains that selling can be seen as the act of getting someone to buy into a concept or an idea, like this one:

Selling: to convince or cause to be accepted.

Example: 'She really sold me on the benefits of not smoking.'

However, the problem with all of these definitions is that they don't really help us as salespeople. That's because each one contains words that could actively lead us in the wrong direction. If we're not careful, words like 'transfer' or 'induce' could lead us to become either transactional or pushy salespeople, neither of which would be good.

So a better definition would be:

Selling is the process of helping someone to make an informed buying decision.

For salespeople, I think this is a much more useful definition for a number of reasons.

- ▶ First, the word *process* steers us away from thinking of a sale as being a simple transaction. It alludes to the fact that selling involves multiple steps or stages *before* the final transaction takes place.

- ▶ Second, the word *helping* is hugely important. Focusing on helping customers is a great way to break down any mental barriers we might have about the sales process. Helpful people are also usually seen as being highly likeable, and customers are much more likely to buy from people they like!

- ▶ Third, the word *informed* helps to indicate that exchanging information is also an important part of selling.

But while this is a much better description, it's not quite enough to be a sales philosophy on its own, because although it alludes to how we might get there, it doesn't actually tell us where we're headed.

Targeting a win-win outcome

In his 1989 book *The Seven Habits of Highly Effective People*, Stephen Covey positions the habit 'think win/win' as a principle of interpersonal leadership. Covey also defines a dimension of win-win interactions as emotional maturity, which he describes as 'the ability to express one's own feelings and convictions, balanced with consideration for the thoughts and feelings of others'.

Those concepts, of win-win thinking and balancing the courage of your convictions with consideration for the other party's needs are ones we can continue to apply to modern-day sales.

Let's explore the various winning and losing options from a sales perspective to understand just why a win-win outcome is best for both sides.

- ▶ **Lose-lose:** If you don't have any courage to actively lead the sales conversation, but also don't have any consideration for the customer's needs, then neither you nor your customer are likely to get any value from the sales process. Both parties will lose, and salespeople in this position might as well not be there at all.

- ▶ **Win-lose:** If you're so full of courage to lead the sales conversation that you don't have any consideration for your customer's needs, then you're into pushy-salesperson territory. Here, you might *think* you're winning at the expense of your customers, but that's usually only the case in the short term. Customers are often quick to realize if they were pushed into a bad buying decision. At best, you end up with an unhappy customer; at worst, you could be on the end of a misselling claim that results in long-term reputational damage.

- ▶ **Lose-win:** Being a pushover and letting your customers win sounds like a bad outcome, but it's probably worse than you think. A lose-win outcome is often what happens when an overly meek or submissive salesperson has high levels of consideration for the customer, but fails to have any courage to take an active role in the conversation. In these cases, just as it was in the last win-lose outcome, customers are equally likely to blame the salesperson for their poor buying decisions if they later realize they didn't get things right. So any perception that the customer 'won' may only be short term.

▶ **Win-win:** All of this explains why greater salespeople balance high levels of consideration for their customers' needs, with high levels of courage to actively lead the sales conversation. They ensure the customer has all the information they need to make a truly informed buying decision, while targeting a win-win outcome that's good for both sides.

This also explains why ambiverts – people who are naturally neither strong introverts nor extraverts but sit somewhere in between – typically make the best salespeople.

Some people still struggle to accept this, believing that extraverts are naturally better salespeople. But in 2008, a meta-analysis of 35 different studies published in the *International Journal of Selection and Assessment* disproved this, when it concluded that there's no link between extraversion and improved sales performance.

The greater sales philosophy

I started this chapter by giving you a better definition of sales, and we've now added the target of a win-win outcome. In doing so, I've also continually referred to sales as being a conversation – a two-way dialogue where you not only need to be considerate of the customer's needs, but you also need to have the courage to actively help the customer to explore and understand why doing something different might be in their best interest. So I've also captured this important principle of exploration in our final sales philosophy. Here it is. The greater sales philosophy is:

**Help customers to make informed buying decisions
by exploring and targeting win-win outcomes.**

Everything you do as a salesperson should be compatible with this statement. This principle should be at the heart of all of your sales conversations, and should guide your sales behaviour at all times. It's something I'll return to throughout this book.

Examples of the greater sales philosophy in practice

Let's look at how our three different sales teams have brought the win-win greater sales philosophy to life by embedding it into their mission statements.

▶ The Drinkit field sales team's mission is to 'help our on-trade and retail customers to sell more beer.' Note that it isn't to help their customers to sell more of Drinkit's beer, or even more non-alcoholic beer, because moving a customer's existing beer sales from one brand to another wouldn't necessarily help the customer to be more profitable. It's only a true win-win if stocking Drinkit's products helps *both* parties to sell more beer as a result.

▶ The SupportIT inside sales team's mission is to 'provide long-term IT support and protection for our customers.' Their customers' win from the support and protection they receive, but it's the 'long-term' nature of the mission statement that's the important win from the sales team's perspective, because longer-term relationships deliver higher profits and higher returns on the upfront sales investment.

▶ The Widget Store sales team's mission is to 'give our customers outstanding buying experiences.' Their customers win from the outstanding experience they receive, and the Widget Store wins because this is specifically phrased as a *buying* experience – outstanding experiences that don't result in a sale don't count.

Why ethical selling is also a win-win

In the introduction to this book, I briefly referenced *morals* as part of the personal performance drivers pyramid when I explained that your moral values define the things that you instinctively believe are right or wrong. How well your natural behaviours align with the sales philosophy we've just explored will, to an extent, depend on your personal moral values.

Ethics are slightly different. They still focus on what's good and bad, or what's right and wrong, but ethics are standards of behaviour that are widely accepted by a large group of similar or loosely connected people. This could be an entire professional sector, or just a group of similar customers.

Businesses, and salespeople, who behave unethically may be penalized by their relevant professional body, or in some cases even by the law. But the real harm often comes from the reputational damage that follows once their customers learn what's been happening. One unethical incident can be sufficient to destroy customer trust in a business. Once trust is broken it can take years to repair and, in some cases, lead to the collapse of a business entirely.

The run on the UK's Northern Rock bank in 2007 is an extreme example. Customers started to withdraw their money after learning about the bank's reckless mortgage sales and lending practices, ultimately leading to the bank's collapse. There are plenty of other examples, too. In 2017 United Airlines suffered a $140 million drop in market value due to a public backlash, after a paying passenger was forcibly removed from a flight because their sales team had oversold tickets. And, in 2025, American Express paid $230 million to settle criminal and civil charges after their sales team were caught misrepresenting fees and rewards for credit cards and other products.

So the impact of unethical selling can be far-reaching indeed.

Defining ethical selling

There isn't a widely accepted definition of ethical selling. This is unfortunate, because having a clear understanding of what customers are likely to see as ethical, rather than what your own personal moral code tells you, can help you to decide what to do in tricky situations. However, we can take inspiration from how the law defines misselling.

In the UK, misselling is illegal under the UK Consumer Protection from Unfair Trading Regulations (2008). These regulations essentially define *misselling* as deliberately or recklessly providing false information; omitting important information; using aggressive sales techniques; or giving incorrect advice as to what the best product or service is for a customer's needs.

If you're selling in the UK, it's important to be aware of this so that you don't fall foul of the law. But we can also use this *misselling* definition to define what most people would see as the desirable opposite: ethical selling.

By taking inspiration from the definition of *misselling*, we can say that ethical salespeople would be widely seen as:

- honest – they don't tell lies;
- truthful – they don't withhold relevant information;
- influential – they use their knowledge and skill to help people to make decisions;

▸ persuasive – they have the courage to debate the merits of their opinions; and

▸ respectful – they never attempt to manipulate or trick people into making specific decisions.

An ethical selling test

Ethical selling is an incredibly nuanced area – one where opinions of precisely what is and what isn't ethical can both change over time, and can be different within different cultures or communities.

So if you are unsure whether an action would be seen as ethical, you can apply this simple test by asking:

▸ (If you were the salesperson concerned) would you feel comfortable explaining your actions to a different prospective customer?

If your honest answer is 'Yes', there's a good chance others would judge that action as being ethical too.

Chapter 1: Summary

The win-win mindset is the belief that the best sales outcomes are those where both the customer and the salesperson benefit.

Here are the key points about what it means to adopt a win-win mindset in sales.

▸ A win-win mindset helps shift your focus from hitting targets to helping customers.

▸ The most effective salespeople balance their courage to lead conversations with genuine consideration for customer's needs.

▸ True selling is a process of actively helping someone make an informed buying decision; it's not facilitating a transaction or pushing someone in a predetermined direction in order to close a deal.

▸ Sales conversations should be guided by a clear philosophy: *help customers explore and target outcomes that work well for both sides*.

▸ Ethical selling, grounded in honesty, respect and transparency, protects your reputation and builds lasting customer trust.

Chapter 2
Is there enough trust?

The trust-builder mindset

The trust-builder mindset is the belief that every sale relies on trust. In the previous chapter we explored why ethical selling is a key part of a win-win sales mindset, but it's also widely considered to be the foundation on which trust is built.

In this chapter we'll build on those foundations as we explore why trust is so important in sales, how it's formed, and how you can build and maintain trust through every interaction you have with your customers.

Why is trust important?

Building and maintaining trust is incredibly important for salespeople. To paraphrase a famous Warren Buffett quote, in sales, trust is like the air you breathe, because you're not going to last long without it.

But what is *trust*? *Trust* is the willingness for someone to put themselves at risk based on their positive belief in another party's motivation, ability and reliability. So trust is required when one person needs or wants something from someone else, but there's a risk of negative consequences if things don't go as well as they hope.

Sales is about getting customers to change and, as you'll learn later in Part 1, customers are naturally biased towards their current situation or *status quo*. So any change away from that is likely to be seen as a risk.

So trust is *always* important. The bigger the change or the risk for the customer, the more trust they're going to need in you, in your brand, and in the products or services you're selling in order to overcome it.

The change-risk-trust link

Let's have a look at some of the changes our different sales teams propose customers make, and the level of risk and trust associated with each one.

The Drinkit sales teams

- ▶ **Proposed change:** A new retail customer starts stocking Drinkit Pale Ale in 300ml bottles, selling it from a shelf or fridge space that's currently under-utilized.

- ▶ **Potential customer risk:** Very low. The only risk is that the initial stock they purchase doesn't sell through and blocks space that could be used to sell another product. However, as the minimum order is just 12 bottles, and there's no obligation for the customer to continue selling the product after that, the financial risk is almost insignificant.

- ▶ **Level of trust required:** Very low.

- ▶ **Proposed change:** A new pub customer starts stocking Drinkit Pale Ale in 20-litre draught kegs in place of a competitor product that currently sells reasonably well.

- ▶ **Potential customer risk:** Medium. If Drinkit Pale Ale doesn't outsell the competitor it replaced, then the customer risks a drop in profit. This could be significant if the rate of sale is below 20 litres per week as, once opened, each keg has a shelf life of just seven days, which means the customer could face additional lost profits due to wastage. There's also a risk of further loss if the consumers who previously drank the competitor product don't like Drinkit's Pale Ale, and choose to drink elsewhere.

- ▶ **Level of trust required:** Medium to high, depending on the rate of sale of the competitor it replaces.

The SupportIT sales team

▸ **Proposed change:** The customer moves from not having access to any specialized IT support to working with SupportIT as their dedicated external IT support partner.

▸ **Potential customer risk:** Variable, depending on how the customer perceives the price and length of contract (higher prices and longer contracts would typically be perceived as higher risk), and the reputation of SupportIT as the external partner who'll receive access to their business-critical data and IT systems.

▸ **Level of trust required:** Variable, but often perceived as significant unless the customer has recently experienced, or is currently experiencing, significant IT issues that they need to resolve.

The Widget sales team

▸ **Proposed change:** A customer purchases a replacement TV for their bedroom, that's manufactured by a brand they know and like, and that's priced within the budget they had in mind.

▸ **Potential customer risk:** Low, as they already trust the brand that manufactures the TV, which also comes with a two-year guarantee and a 30-day no-quibble return option.

▸ **Level of trust required:** Low, but likely to increase the more the customer sees their new TV as being different from one they're already familiar with. In which case, the customer will likely need more trust in the salesperson and the advice they give in order to overcome the perceived increased risk.

▸ **Proposed change:** A customer purchases a replacement TV for their bedroom that's manufactured by a brand they're not familiar with and, because of the additional features it comes with, is priced above the budget they had in mind.

▸ **Potential customer risk:** Medium. Although the TV still comes with a guarantee, there's still a risk that they won't like the user experience it provides, or won't end up using the additional features that justified its premium price.

▸ **Level of trust required:** Medium.

As you can see from these examples, different proposed changes carry different levels of potential risk for the customer, and so require different levels of trust. In short: the more a customer has to change, the more trust you need to earn to offset their sense of risk.

The neuroscience of trust

Humans are naturally inclined to trust others, but we don't always. Experiments by Paul J. Zak, professor in Neuroscience at Claremont Graduate University, have shown that the key to this is oxytocin. Oxytocin is often called the love hormone because it's released by our brains when we feel safe and connected to others, and biologically fosters feelings of bonding and trust.

Higher levels of oxytocin in our brains:

- increases our empathy;

- reduces our fear of strangers;

- increases our generosity;

- makes it more likely we'll cooperate and reciprocate;

- makes us more forgiving;

- drives social engagement; and

- encourages loyalty through repeated exposure.

In short, oxytocin drives trust and, as I'm sure you'll agree from that list of outcomes, it encourages positive behaviours that you want from your customers.

The enemy of trust is stress. Most people know this intuitively, because when we feel nervous or stressed, we don't usually interact well with others. This is because stress triggers our bodies to release hormones that are potent oxytocin inhibitors – chemicals that block oxytocin and effectively reverse its effects.

So, stress...

- decreases our empathy;

- increases our fear of strangers;

- decreases our generosity;

- makes it less likely we'll cooperate and reciprocate;

- makes us less forgiving;

- reduces social engagement; and

- reduces feelings of loyalty

… which are all negative behaviours you don't want to encourage!

So in order to build and maintain trust, you need to do things that trigger the release of oxytocin in your customers' brains, and avoid things that might make them feel nervous or overly stressed.

Secrets to building and maintaining trust

Trust takes effort to build and maintain but it's easy to break and, once broken, it's often incredibly difficult to repair. But with the right mindset many of the actions required to build and maintain trust should come naturally, especially after you've read this book.

You've already started to learn about the first three secrets to building and maintaining trust in the previous chapter. Here's a recap.

- **Be transparent.** Be open about why the sale you're proposing is good for you too;

- **Be honest.** Don't bend the truth or tell lies, and don't withhold relevant information; and

- **Don't manipulate.** Use your knowledge and skills to influence customers, and have the courage to persuade them through active debate where necessary, but never attempt to trick them into a sale.

In the next chapter you're going to learn about the fourth secret. Here's a brief outline.

- **Add value.** People have a tendency to evaluate interactions and relationships based on the value they provide, and we're naturally more trusting of people who focus on our own needs and wants as well as theirs.

The next two secrets to building and maintaining trust are aspects we'll explore in more detail in Part 2, when we'll look at how to:

> ▷ **Be credible** – by having a deep understanding of what you're selling.

> ▷ **Demonstrate commitment** – by actively looking after customers through every step of their buying journey.

Then, in Part 3, you're going to learn the New 7-Step Sale, the steps of which are designed to build and maintain trust as you guide customers through a natural-feeling sales conversation. The trust-building secrets embedded into those seven steps are as follows.

> ▷ **Be authentic.** You'll learn more about the importance and practicality of being genuine and authentic as part of Step 2 of the sales process: Engage your customer.

> ▷ **Build a connection.** This trust driver is embedded throughout the seven-step sales process, but you'll focus on it specifically as part of Step 3: Understand your customer; and Step 4: Propose and present.

> ▷ **Be clear.** People tend to distrust information that's ambiguous or difficult to understand. So in Step 4 – Propose and present – I'll show you how to craft and deliver sales messages that are clear and succinct.

> ▷ **Be similar.** People like to buy from people like them. So in Step 4 I'll also show you how you can be similar to your customers while remaining authentic to your true self as you propose and present your recommendations.

> ▷ **Show care and compassion.** Although it may come as a surprise, this is an important part of Step 5 of the sales process: Handle and overcome objections.

> ▷ **Be consistent.** Give all of your customers a consistently great buying experience throughout their entire interaction with you and your organization. This includes staying consistent with your beliefs and opinions as you handle objections, or move to compromise through negotiation if your attempt to overcome their objection fails.

> ▷ **Be reliable and accountable.** You'll look at how to do this as part of Step 7 of the sales process: Follow-up.

Chapter 2: Summary

The trust-builder mindset is the belief that every sale depends on trust, and a salesperson's role is to build and maintain trust to help their customers to overcome real and perceived risks, and make a positive change.

Trust-building starts with adopting the right mindset. Here are the key principles we covered in this chapter that will help you to do that.

- Trust is vital in sales because every sale involves a level of risk and change for the customer.

- The greater the perceived risk or change, the more trust the customer will need in you, your brand and your proposed solution.

- Neuroscience shows that trust is influenced by the hormone oxytocin, which is *triggered* when people feel safe, connected and supported, and *blocked* when they feel stressed.

- To build trust, avoid creating stress and, instead, focus on behaviours that foster empathy, connection and loyalty.

- Many of the mindsets in Part 1 and the knowledge areas in Part 2 of this book are directly linked to trust-building behaviours.

- In Part 3 you'll discover how to use the New 7-Step Sale to embed trust-building actions naturally into every sales conversation.

Chapter 3
Are you adding enough value?

The value-add mindset

In Chapters 1 and 2 we looked at the importance of targeting win-win outcomes and building and maintaining trust, but that's not all you need to help your customers to make an informed buying decision. Customers will only buy what you're selling if they believe they're going to benefit from it.

A *value-add* mindset involves more than just providing information or signposting customers towards the more easily recognized benefits of your products or services. Salespeople with a value-add mindset believe their role is to add value to customers through every step of the sales process.

This is important because, as I mentioned in the previous chapter, people have a natural tendency to evaluate interactions and relationships based on their net value, comparing the benefits they receive (which can include emotional as well as more practical or material benefits) to the costs they incur in exchange (such as time, effort, money or cognitive and emotional strain).

This principle of Social Exchange Theory is a widely accepted tenet of all social interactions, but it particularly applies to sales, where both sides are often motivated by self-interest, but are also particularly sensitive to the principles of balance and fairness.

So if part of your role is to add value, let's move on to look at how customers perceive and judge the value that brands, products and salespeople add.

Understanding what customers value

When it comes to how we view the world, we all have the following.

- ▶ **Foundational and idealistic values.** These represent how we believe the world should be.

- ▶ **Rational and pragmatic needs.** These usually relate to current problems we'd like to solve.

- ▶ **Emotional and subjective wants.** These are based on (or for business customers, are at least heavily influenced by) our personal feelings, tastes and opinions.

Our values (which are different from our concept of *value*) remain largely consistent over time and across different situations. They're the principles and ideals that we live by.

Our needs are contextual. They relate to a specific topic, situation or set of circumstances. They range from our silent expectations – needs we expect to be met by the products or services we buy and so don't tend to talk or ask about. The need for the product being advertised to be available is often a good example of a silent expectation – we expect it to be, and so we wouldn't typically ask a salesperson about its availability without good reason.

At the other end of our needs spectrum sit our motivational needs. These are needs we recognize as being more difficult to meet, and so are more motivated to actively seek out products or services that might satisfy them. Long-lasting batteries are a good example of a motivational need. Whether you own an electric vehicle or a smart phone, if it's often out of charge when you need it you're likely to be motivated to find a better alternative.

Our wants are more transient because they're usually driven by emotional responses to things that are different or unexpected. The things we want the most are often things that are particularly rare, new or innovative. But over time, as these things become more commonplace or we simply get used to them being around, those emotions tend to subside.

This idea is adapted from the Kano model of customer satisfaction. Together, these values, needs and wants form the mental and emotional lens through which we view and evaluate any product or service. You can see this represented in the pyramid-shaped diagram in Figure 2, which has our foundational values on the bottom layer, our rational needs in the middle, and our more emotional wants at the top.

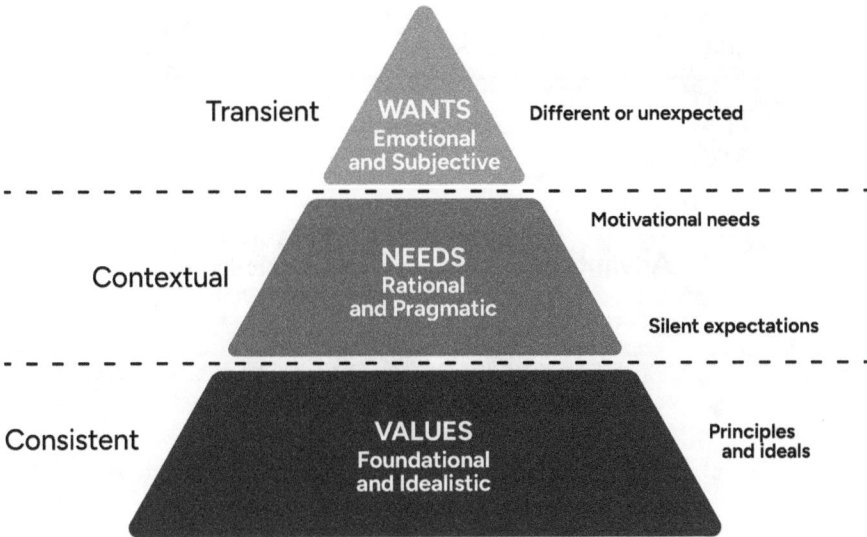

Transient — WANTS / Emotional and Subjective — Different or unexpected

Motivational needs

Contextual — NEEDS / Rational and Pragmatic

Silent expectations

Consistent — VALUES / Foundational and Idealistic — Principles and ideals

Figure 2: The values, needs and wants lens

Customers value brands that align with their personal values and ideals, they value products and services that satisfy their rational needs and emotional wants, and they value salespeople who do all of these things.

We're going to look more deeply at how a value-add mindset should impact how you think and act shortly. But first, let's look more closely at how the products and services you sell, add value for your customers.

The FAB cycle: Linking features to benefits

Customers value products and services that satisfy their rational needs and emotional wants. So demonstrating value involves explicitly linking the features of your products and services to the benefits they provide in these areas.

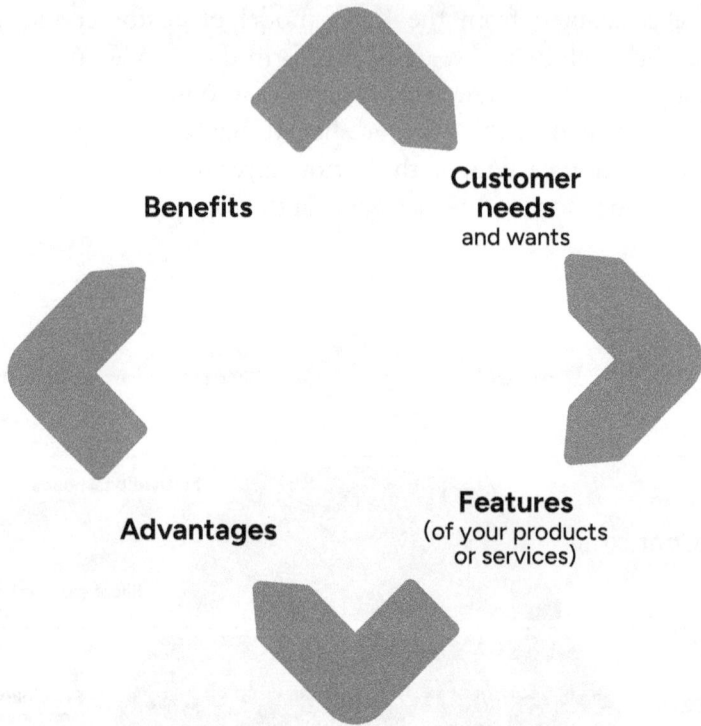

Figure 3: The features, advantages and benefits cycle

Take a look at Figure 3. As the features, advantages and benefits – or 'FAB' cycle – illustrates, the basic premise behind selling a product or service is that it's possible to identify groups of customers with similar needs. When that happens, organizations design products or services that include features to satisfy those needs.

We're going to explore the features of your products or services in more detail in Part 2, when we'll look at just what it is you're selling. So for now, just recognize that a feature is something a product or service has, is, does, or comes with. While the value of the feature might be subjective, a feature is factual – it's something that everyone would agree exists.

In addition to designing products and services with features that satisfy needs customers know they have, innovative organizations also develop features that customers didn't know they 'needed' – until they knew about them. These types of 'need' are better described as 'wants', and they're why the arrow that sits between customer needs and features in the FAB cycle diagram points both ways. Innovative features can cause customers to have needs, just as customer needs can cause organizations to develop features to satisfy them.

The advantages of features can be explained and understood by anyone. But, and this is the important part, they *only* benefit an individual customer if they satisfy their *personal* needs or wants. This personalization is important. It's also something that separates sales from marketing.

Due to the broadcast nature of the channels they use, marketers tend to speak to large groups of customers at once. Because of this, marketers typically have to select what they believe will be the most relevant product or service for a group of customers they can reach, and then describe its key features and advantages in a way they hope will resonate.

This is not me talking-down our marketing colleagues, because getting this even halfway right takes a lot of skill, as does not alienating prospective customers by sending the wrong messages. I'm sure the possibilities for personalized marketing will continue to improve as customer data and digital tools get even better. But for now, salespeople have an advantage that marketers don't. We typically have interactive conversations with individual customers, which enables us to adapt and personalize our messages in the moment to maximize their effectiveness.

Because we communicate with individual customers, as salespeople we can take the time to tease out and diagnose each customer's specific needs, and listen carefully to how *they* describe them. Not only can we then be sure we're going to recommend our most suitable product or service, but also we can describe it in a uniquely personalized way by highlighting the specific features and advantages that will benefit this particular customer, using words and stories that we're confident will resonate with them strongly.

This is a concept that we're going to build on as you move through this book. In Part 2 we'll explore the features, advantages and benefits of your products and services when we explore what you're selling in more detail. Then in Part 3, you'll learn what you need to do to put this into action, and have highly personalized and effective sales conversations with your prospects and customers.

But for now, I want you to focus on three things.

1. Customers value products and services that satisfy their rational needs and emotional wants.

2. It's the features of the product or service that provide these benefits, not the product or service itself.

3. Value is subjective, not just because different types of customers will have different needs, but because customers are different *people*. The value customers place on brands, products, services, *and salespeople* will be impacted, at least in part, by their *personal* values, views and emotions.

A *note on customer values*

The FAB cycle involves linking features to benefits in order to satisfy a customer's needs and wants, but it doesn't explicitly explain how products and services link to a customer's values and ideals.

This is because our value-based desires tend to be satisfied by the brands we buy into and the organizations we buy from, rather than by products or services themselves.

These brand-values can be considered to be features in their own right, and so they can, and in some cases should, form part of your sales conversations. But when this happens it's usually because a brand-value is so important to a particular customer that they consider it to be one of their needs or wants. We'll come back to this in Part 3, when I'll explain how to understand what an individual customer needs and wants, and what you need to do in response.

A *quick example*

Before we move on to explore how salespeople add value, let's look at a quick example of how a customer's values, needs and wants might align with a brand's values and the features of one of its products. I'm going to choose Apple, because it's a brand you're likely to be familiar with.

▶   **Values.** Apple's values include innovation, simplicity, accessibility, and privacy. So customers whose values align with these principles tend to be drawn towards its products and services.

▶   **Needs.** Even though, when Apple first launched their iPhone, there were audible gasps from the audience when Steve Jobs demoed its touch screen, the absence of physical buttons is no longer something that excites customers. What was once an exciting and new innovation has become something customers now *silently expect* all phones to offer.

But a customer who's concerned about information security might be more *motivated* to buy an iPhone because they could *benefit* from its security features. Apple's closed ecosystem, regular updates and vetted App Store, means their phones are typically less susceptible to hacking or malware than those of their competitors.

▷ **Wants.** Creating new and innovative features that customers want is where Apple often shines. While their latest innovation might not fulfil a rational and pragmatic need that consumers would have identified before it was launched, that doesn't make them want it any less once it becomes available. Afterall, we all like 'new and shiny' things, especially when they align with the values we hold dear.

How salespeople add value

Your customers can probably buy what you're selling without you. Even if your organization doesn't provide channels that they can buy through without interacting with you as a salesperson, your competitors *do*. So if you're going to be in the loop, you've *got* to add value.

As I explained at the start of this chapter, a value-add mindset involves more than just providing information or signposting customers towards the more easily recognizable benefits of your products or services. So as a salesperson, how should you add value?

The answer to that question could be a very long list, but here are the essential value-add principles you need to embrace.

▷ **Help customers make good buying decisions.** As you learnt in Chapter 1, a salesperson's role is to help customers to make informed buying decisions by exploring and targeting win-win outcomes. Not only does this involve taking time to understand and consider the customer's wants and needs, but this also involves having the courage to actively lead the sale and prevent customers from making buying decisions they might later regret.

▷ **Help customers to recognize their unknown needs.** Often customers will know what they need, but great salespeople also help customers to explore things they maybe haven't considered. As Henry Ford, founder of the Ford Motor Company, apparently once said, 'If I had asked people what they wanted, they would have said faster horses.'

▶ **Help customers to recognize hidden benefits.** Just as some customers may not recognize some of their needs or wants, many won't know about some of the features of your product or service, or recognize how they could benefit them.

▶ **Save customers' time.** Customers can probably discover everything they need to know about your brand and product or service online. But the internet is a big place, and it's a lot quicker to find the answers you're looking for if you have a guide that knows you well.

▶ **Provide expert advice.** Good salespeople offer choices. Greater salespeople use their knowledge, experience and expertise to reduce decision-making effort by recommending the *best* way forward.

▶ **Save customers money.** This isn't necessarily about giving customers access to discounts or being able to negotiate lower prices for higher volume deals. Advising a customer *not* to buy something they don't really need, or to save money by buying a lower-priced option that meets all of their requirements, is a great way to add value, trust and loyalty, which can pay dividends in the long run.

▶ **Challenge customers to think differently.** Most people have friends who mainly think like they do, which is why social media is often described as an echo chamber. But if they do what everyone else is doing, they're just going to get the average results everyone else is getting. Great salespeople challenge customers to think differently and help them to receive greater benefits – realizing greater results.

▶ **Provide support throughout the customer's journey.** The customer journey starts with awareness – of their needs or problems, or of you, your brand, or your potential solutions. It continues through the prospective and active customer phases, potentially to the point when they eventually become a lapsed customer. Regardless of whether they do so directly or indirectly, great salespeople can support customers and add value at every stage.

You'll learn more about all of these value-add principles, and how to put them into action, through the remainder of this book.

Chapter 3: Summary

The value-add mindset is the belief that a salesperson's role is to bring meaningful benefits to customers at every step of the sales process. Not just by providing information, but by actively helping them to make better decisions, to discover hidden value, and to feel more confident about their choices.

Here are the key points to take away from this chapter about how to develop and apply your value-add mindset.

- ▶ Customers judge value by weighing the benefits they receive against the effort, cost or strain involved to achieve them.

- ▶ Understanding what customers value involves considering how the benefits you provide align with the customer's foundational values, rational needs and emotional wants.

- ▶ Greater salespeople add value by guiding customers through informed decision making – uncovering hidden needs, highlighting overlooked benefits, and offering expert, trustworthy advice.

- ▶ Greater salespeople also save customers' time, reduce decision-making effort, and provide ongoing support throughout the buying journey – often challenging customers to think differently and achieve better outcomes.

- ▶ There are many ways you can add value, but the fundamental principle is to treat every customer as an individual and focus on providing personalized help.

Chapter 4
What's their gut feeling?

The decision-focused mindset

In the previous chapter we began to explore how customers might make a decision to buy your product or service based on the *value* it could provide. We did this by considering how its features align with their needs and wants.

In this chapter we'll build on that by exploring why the decision to buy or not buy what you're selling is only one of many relevant decisions your customers make. Your customers will make decisions as a result of *every* conversation you have, and regardless of whether either of you recognize it or not, those decisions will be both numerous and nuanced.

Some of their decisions and decision-making processes will be obvious, but many may not be, and that's where the gut comes in. Asking yourself what the customer's gut is feeling can help to illuminate aspects of their decision-making that might otherwise remain hidden.

The decision-focused mindset is about recognizing all of this, and focusing on helping customers to make all of their many buying decisions as efficiently and effectively as possible.

How people think they make decisions

If you're going to help people to make decisions, you need to understand how the decision-making process works. Because the closer you align your sales conversations and selling messages with how your customers make decisions, the more successful you'll be.

If you ask a professional buyer about the purchasing process they go through, they'll often describe it as having five different stages.

1. **Need recognition.** The buyer recognizes they have a need that's not being met.

2. **Search for information.** The buyer seeks out information about different possible solutions.

3. **Evaluation of alternatives.** The buyer evaluates the different solutions available to their problem.

4. **Buying decision.** The buyer chooses the product or service they believe will best meet their need.

5. **Post-purchase evaluation.** The buyer evaluates whether they made the right decision.

Regardless of whether you recognize that as a process your customers go through or not, it doesn't even scratch the surface of what's truly happening when anyone makes a buying decision.

Customers and salespeople often think of a buying decision as being just that, a single decision that someone has made to buy, or not buy, a product or service. But whether either party realizes it or not, the customer journey is actually one that involves many decisions.

For example, here are some of the many different decisions and questions a customer might face before they make any final decision to buy what you're selling.

▶ Should I change what I'm currently doing? What would the benefit be?

▶ Should I make this change now? Is this urgent, or could it wait?

▶ What's the best type of solution? Or, is *this* the best type of solution?

▶ Which company should I buy from? Or, is *this* the right company to buy from?

▶ Which specific product or service is right for me? Or, is *this* the right product or service for me?

- ▶ Is it worth paying that price? Will I get enough value in return?

- ▶ Can I afford it? Do I have sufficient money, cashflow or budget?

- ▶ Which sales channel should I buy through? Or, should I buy from this salesperson, or would I be better buying another way?

My point is that whatever your customer's journey looks like, I guarantee it involves them making far more than just one decision. But while this takes us closer to how buying decisions are really made, it still doesn't cover everything that's going on.

How people really make decisions

When we're making a decision, we like to think we do so consciously. We might take our time and put deliberate effort into the process, carefully thinking through all of the different factors like the ones I listed in the previous section – especially if we're making a complex decision. But the problem is that while to an extent that's true, it's not all that's going on. As Professor Daniel Kahneman explains in his book *Thinking, Fast and Slow*, this part of our thinking is only the second of two types of process in our brain. There's another aspect to our thinking and decision making too, which he calls system-one.

While system-two processes are conscious, slow, effortful and good for making complex decisions, system-one processes are subconscious, fast, automatic and good for making every-day decisions.

To understand why we have two systems, think about what happens when you learn to drive. To start with, everything is deliberate and rational, but over time driving becomes second nature, to such an extent that you probably only engage system-two thinking in new or complex situations. But once these become familiar every-day occasions, system-one processes develop to take over, and you start making decisions about what to do quickly and automatically, without even realizing you're doing it. The problem is that once a system-one process gets activated, there's very little you can do to stop it.

You can experience this in action for yourself using the Stroop Test. In this test, different words are displayed on a screen and respondents are challenged to say the colour the word is written in out loud, as quickly as possible. This is easy to do when the word has nothing to do with the colour of the font it's written in. For example, if I showed you the word 'cat' written in a green font, you'd probably find it easy to quickly say 'green'. It's also easy to do when the word and its font colour are the same. But if I chose a blue font to display the word 'red', when challenged to react quickly, most people tend to shout out 'red' rather than the correct answer of 'blue'.

The reason most people get this wrong at first is because they've developed a system-one process that's very fast at recognizing the word 'red', so it tends to get to that answer much more quickly than their system-two, which is busy processing the new skill of separating the colour of the font from the word itself.

If you want to try the Stroop Test, you'll find a video on my website at greatersales.com/bookextras.

Why all customers are biased

As the learning-to-drive example illustrates, our brains have developed the ability to create these mental short-cuts in order to ease the burden of the many thousands of decisions we have to make each day. Psychologists call these short-cuts *heuristics* or *cognitive biases*, and without them humans simply wouldn't have evolved into the successful species we've become. Think of how many micro-decisions you make each time you prepare and eat a meal for example, and how paralyzingly slow and difficult it would be if you had to consciously make each of these decisions separately.

Psychologists have now identified many hundreds of these decision-making short-cuts. Here are a few that are likely to impact the decisions your customers make.

> ▸ **The status quo bias.** This emotional bias manifests as a preference for the current state of affairs. The current situation (or the status quo) is taken as a reference point and any change away from that baseline is perceived as a loss or a risk. Even if the current situation isn't good and the alternative is likely to be an improvement, most people have a natural bias towards 'better the devil you know' when making decisions.

> ▸ **The halo effect.** This cognitive bias explains why positive impressions of people, brands, and products in one area, can positively influence our feelings in another. For example, we're more likely to believe that good-looking people are kind, honest

and intelligent; that confident people are competent; and that products manufactured by successful brands will successfully meet our needs.

▷ **The loss aversion bias.** This cognitive bias explains why we're more likely to be motivated into action by the thought of losing something, than we are by the thought of gaining something we don't yet have. But loss aversion can kick-in even if we just think that we might lose something in the future. This is why FOMO (the fear of missing out) is a powerful motivator, because our instinct is also to avoid potential pain from a future loss.

If the psychology of decision-making is something that specifically interests you, I've listed a few great books on this subject in the bibliography at the end of this book.

Developing your decision-focused mindset

Here are five things you need to focus on to develop your decision-focused mindset.

1. As a salesperson you can always impact customer decisions to some degree. Because system-one thinking is automatic and subconscious, even when customers or professional buyers *believe* they're following a logical decision-making process, they're much more open to influence than they might expect.

2. Even professional psychologists can't follow exactly what's going on inside a customer's brain as they make a buying decision, so you shouldn't expect to! But you need to recognize that even though neither you nor your customer can hear them, their hidden system-one decision-maker is always chipping in. So you've got to appeal to both their logical system-two (their rational thinking), *and* their more biased system-one (their intuitive 'gut' reactions). For example, it's not just what you say to customers but also how you make them feel. Your customers will base their buying decision on their whole experience, not just your logically justified proposal.

3. Although every customer is different, we've all evolved similar ways of biased thinking. So doing certain things in certain ways is likely to improve your chances of success. But because

decision-making is a personalized and nuanced process, we all perceive things slightly differently, so there are no guarantees. Things that usually work well won't work every time, which is why selling isn't easy – it takes skill. You need to follow proven sales techniques, but you also need to read, respond and adapt to the customer in front of you. (I'll show you how to do both of those things in Part 3.)

4. Even once you think, know and do everything that's in this book, you're still going to regularly get told 'no' by your customers. Partly because it's pointless to set yourself objectives that are easy to achieve every time, but also because decision-making is complex to understand and impossible to fully control for all the reasons we've explored in this chapter. This is why sales is as much about how you handle failure as it is about how you strive for success. You need to aim for *yeses*, but accept that you're going to hear a lot of *noes* along the way.

5. Despite accepting that *yeses* can't be guaranteed, you mustn't let that put you off. Your underlying objective is to help your customer to make an informed buying decision by exploring and *targeting* a win-win outcome – so you've *got* to drive your sales conversations towards a decision.

Chapter 4: Summary

The decision-focused mindset is the belief that customers don't just make one big decision to buy or not, but instead make many small and often subconscious decisions throughout their buying journey – and that a salesperson's role is to help them make each one as easily and effectively as possible.

Here are the key ideas to take away from this chapter to help you develop your decision-focused mindset.

▸ Customers make many nuanced decisions throughout the buying process – not just a single 'yes' or 'no'.

▸ These decisions are shaped by both logical thinking, *and* by fast automatic reactions that are driven by mental short-cuts or biases.

▸ Helping customers to make decisions means focusing on what they think *and* how they feel.

▶ You can't understand or control everything that impacts a customer's decision, and so you'll still hear 'no' often – resilience is key.

▶ There are always things you can do to tip the needle of probability in your favour.

▶ Your role is to actively guide your customer towards making a well-informed, win-win decision.

Chapter 5

Is this the best

investment for you?

The return-on-investment (or ROI) mindset

We added weight to the customer side of the win-win mindset through the belief that you should always seek to add value for the customer. The ROI mindset balances this because it explains that you should always seek to maximize the value you and your organization receive, too.

The return on investment (or ROI) principle explains that whenever you invest something, be it your time, money or any other finite resource, you're doing so because you want to get something back in return. If the return you get out, or the profit you make, is worth more than the investment you put in to generate it, that's a positive outcome (or a positive return on investment).

But just as it is with sales and buying decisions, profits aren't always guaranteed either. With any investment there's always a risk that the return you get out won't outweigh the investment you put in to try to generate it. That, of course, would be a negative outcome (or a negative return on investment).

But even if you're confident your investment *will* generate a positive return, any resources you invest in one area are usually then tied up, at least for a period of time, which means they can't be invested elsewhere.

So the ROI mindset is about prioritization. It involves evaluating different options and actions based on their potential to generate a positive return. It's the principle that whenever you have time, money or any other type of finite or costly resource, you shouldn't think about using or spending it. You should focus on *investing* it wherever it's likely to deliver a maximum return.

Working with finite and costly resources

Let's explore the finite and costly resources that our three different sales teams have available to invest.

The Drinkit sales team

Their finite resources include their time and attention, plus various printed sales aids. But they also have access to some items that cost a lot more and so are in much more limited supply, including hospitality tickets for prestigious shows and sporting events. Because of their high cost, they have to choose carefully where and when to invest these if they're going to maximize their chances of generating a positive return on investment.

They also have a wide range of sales support resources they can invest to help win new customers and drive existing customers' sales by negotiating new product listings in return for an enhanced package of support.

These additional resources include free start-up stock and branded glassware; printed point-of-sale (or 'POS' material) to drive visibility and awareness; more premium POS materials such as branded parasols and staff polo shirts; and the resources and additional free stock needed to run consumer promotions such as 'buy one get one free'. They're also able to invest additional time to help improve their rate of sale in existing customer accounts, including by running free training sessions for customer staff and free sampling events for shoppers and drinkers.

Each of these additional resources has a financial cost, including the salesperson's time. This means each member of the Drinkit sales team has a finite budget to work with each year, which limits the amounts they can use.

The SupportIT sales team

The SupportIT sales team's finite resources primarily consist of their time and attention, but they also have a small range of items provided by their marketing team to help them win new clients. These include printed mailers that they can post, which are very low-cost and so are only finite in principle.

On occasion they may have access to higher-cost items such as hospitality tickets. But these are usually reserved for use by SupportIT's customer care team, who are tasked with retaining and growing customer accounts after the sales team have brought them in and handed them over.

The Widget Store's sales team

The Widget Store's sales team's finite resources are simply their time and attention. Any time and attention they invest with one customer can't be invested with another who might also be browsing the shop floor, struggling to make a buying decision. So despite the fact they don't have access to any additional sales resources, it's still important that they focus on how they invest this finite and costly resource wisely.

Calculating your investment cost

Obviously, I don't know everything that's in the toolkit of resources you can invest to generate a return in the form of new, retained or increased sales, nor what any of those resources cost. But it's important that *you* do.

Typically, though, the most finite, costly and under-valued resource that every salesperson has available to invest is their time. So let's explore how much the time you invest in order to generate a sale can cost.

I'm going to walk you through a calculation, but if you're not yet confident with numbers, don't worry. I'm going to explain the process first, and then I'll give you a worked example for one of our sales teams, which you can plug your own numbers into if you wish.

But it's the principles rather than the numbers that are most important, and I've summarized those for you at the end of this chapter. So this isn't necessarily a calculation you have to do for yourself.

How to calculate your sales-time investment costs

Step 1: Start with your base annual salary.

Step 2: To convert this into your true annual cost, you need to factor in all of the other costs that are directly associated with your employment.

These include any taxes, social security or pension contributions your employer has to pay on top of your salary; any sales bonus they pay you; the cost of providing and running your company car if you have one; costs associated with the IT equipment, software and phone you use; costs for any external training, meetings or events you attend; any additional work-related expenses that you claim; *plus* a share of the direct cost of your sales management team.

The reason you'll probably have to include a proportion of your line-manager's costs is because unless they independently generate sales themselves, the existence of their role is directly related to that of yours and your teammates. So their costs must also be covered by the sales their team collectively generates, before the remaining profit can be passed on to the rest of the business.

This step sounds complicated to calculate, but after running these numbers with lots of different sales teams, once all of those elements have been factored in, the true annual cost for most frontline salespeople ends up being around 2.5 times their base salary.

Calculate your true annual cost by multiplying your base salary by 2.5.

Step 3: Next, we need to calculate your cost per sales day.

To do this you need to work out how many days a year you directly invest in generating sales. So from the 365 days that are theoretically available, you need to deduct: all of the weekends and public holidays that you don't work; the total number of days of paid leave that you're given; the average number of sick days you take each year; plus any days you spend at work when you're not directly making sales, such as days for training or company events. Once you have that number:

Calculate your cost per sales day by dividing your true annual cost from Step 2 by your number of selling days per year.

Step 4: Next, we need to calculate your cost per sales call or visit.

To do this you need to know the average number of sales calls or visits you make each day you dedicate to sales activities. This number might be tracked and calculated for you, because for many sales teams it's one of their input KPIs. But if this number isn't something that your organization tracks, I strongly recommend that you track it for yourself. For the purpose of this calculation you ideally want to use your daily average across a whole year. Once you know the average number of sales calls or visits you make per sales day:

Calculate your cost per call or visit by dividing your daily cost from Step 3 by the average number of calls or visits you make per sales day.

Step 5: Finally, we need to calculate your cost per sale.

To do this you need to know your sales conversion rate, which is the percentage of sales calls or visits you make that result in a sale.

To calculate that, first work out how many sales calls or visits you make per year. You can do that by multiplying the average number you make per day (from Step 4), by your number of sales days per year (from Step 3). Then, take the total number of sales you make each year (which needs to be the number of individual sales you make, not the value generated by those sales), and divide it by the annual sales calls or visits number you've just calculated.

That will give you your sales call or visit conversion rate expressed as a percentage. So an answer of 0.1 would indicate you have a 10% conversion rate: 10% of the calls or visits you make result in a sale. Once you've calculated your conversion rate, to complete this step:

Calculate your cost per sale, by multiplying your cost per call from Step 4 by your sales conversion rate percentage expressed as a decimal.

The final figure from Step 5 represents how much you cost your organization for each sale you make. But this excludes the cost of any additional sales resources you invest along the way, such as the POS materials and hospitality tickets that the Drinkit sales team use in the example earlier. So in order to calculate your total customer acquisition cost you'd need to factor those in too.

Let's look at an example to see how that might all stack up.

A worked example for the Drinkit on-trade sales team

Let's see how much it costs the Drinkit company for each new customer their on-trade sales team bring in, starting with the cost of the sales time they invest.

Step 1:	Take the average salesperson's base annual salary		=	£40,000
Step 2:	× 2.5 (for additional employment costs, as explained earlier)	= cost per year	=	£100,000
Step 3:	÷ 220 (a Drinkit salesperson's selling days per year)	= cost per day	=	£454.55
Step 4:	÷ 12 (average sales visits per Drinkit salesperson per day)	= cost per visit	=	£37.88
Step 5:	÷ 8.4% (0.084) (their average sales conversion rate)	= cost per sale	=	£450.94

If we round that final number to the nearest pound, that tells us that on average, for each new sale the Drinkit on-trade sales team makes, the time they invest to generate it costs the Drinkit company £451.

But to get to the total new customer acquisition cost they also need to add on the cost of any additional sales resources they invest into that new customer, plus any costs directly associated with getting that customer up and running.

For Drinkit's on-trade sales team, not only do these customer onboarding and activation costs include POS materials, glassware and a small amount of start-up stock, but Drinkit also have to pay for a new draught beer font to be installed onto the customer's bar. For the Drinkit on-trade sales team, these additional customer onboarding and activation costs average out at £299 per new customer.

When this is added to the £451 it costs for the salesperson's time, this gives the Drinkit on-trade sales team a total customer acquisition cost of £750 per new draught beer customer – which is a significant amount of money!

Generating a return on investment

A cost only becomes an investment if the intention is to directly generate a positive return, and a positive return on investment is one where what's returned is worth more than the investment put in to generate it.

In the previous example, Drinkit typically only breaks even on a sale once a customer has purchased stock that generates £750 in profits. As Drinkit makes a gross profit of £10 on each keg they sell, that means a new customer has to buy more than 75 kegs of beer in order for Drinkit to begin to get a positive return on their sales investment. Any less than that, and their negative return on investment will mean they've lost money.

As Drinkit's average pub customer only sells 1.5 kegs of their beer each week, this means it typically takes just under a year before each new customer starts to become profitable. So you can see why the Drinkit on-trade sales team are also charged with retaining and growing existing customer accounts, as well as prospecting and winning new ones!

This example, like the previous calculations, focuses on the *financial* aspects of ROI. Whenever you're calculating the financial ROI of any sales activity, the cost of any investments that failed to generate a positive return needs to be covered by those that did. This is why Step 5 of the previous calculation divides the salesperson's annual costs over only the conversations that resulted in a sale, because the profits from those sales need to cover *all* of the salesperson's costs in order to generate a positive ROI overall.

But while financial measures are usually the most important and easiest way to calculate ROI from sales activities, money should not be the only focus for your ROI mindset. For example, it would be difficult to calculate the financial ROI generated by a case study gained from a widely respected customer in return for simply asking for permission to share their story. But a case study can be an incredibly valuable resource when it comes to overcoming objections and closing sales, even if it would be difficult to quantify exactly how much it helped in the context of the whole conversation.

Similarly, an unsuccessful sales conversation can generate at least *some* return, if what you learn from it helps you to improve the conversations you have with other prospects and customers. Again, the financial return would be very hard to quantify, but you shouldn't discount the value of learning from failure altogether.

Maximizing your return on investment

The previous Drinkit example shows just how important – and potentially how difficult – it is to deliver a positive return on investment, and just how quickly costs could add up if you don't get things right. So any steps you can take to maximize your ROI can be very valuable indeed.

Traditional thinking says there are three things you can do to try to improve your return on investment.

1. You can increase the likelihood that your actions will generate a positive return.

2. You can increase the size of the return you're likely to get.

3. You can reduce the investment you put in to try to generate it.

But maximizing your return on investment this way needs a balanced approach.

▶ If you try to maximize the size of your return by chasing bigger customers, you might have to increase the amount of time and other resources you invest into the process. But your likelihood of success, and therefore your overall ROI, might actually *decrease* if those big fish are attracting the attention of your significant competitors too.

▶ If you try to maximize your chances of success by chasing lots of smaller customers who might be quicker and easier to win and might require less investment to do so, the size of the return you get from each one is likely to be smaller. So you're going to need to win many more of them in order to increase the ROI you deliver.

▶ If you try to improve your ROI by reducing the investment you put in, which in sales terms typically means investing less time and money into the process, you might find this reduces the likelihood that your actions will produce a return at all.

So if you're not careful, that traditional way of thinking can tie you in knots and lead to over-thinking or 'analysis paralysis', which can dissuade you from making any changes in one area for fear of negative consequences in another.

In frontline sales, rather than trying to follow that traditional line of thinking, I believe a better way to maximize your ROI is to focus on four areas that you should always try to increase or improve. These are your sales efficiency, effectiveness, consistency and volume. I'll explain why in the next chapter, when I'll also show you how even small improvements in these areas can generate incredible results.

Chapter 5: Summary

The return-on-investment (or ROI) mindset is the belief that every use of your time, money or other finite resources should be treated as an investment – carefully evaluated and prioritized to generate the greatest possible return.

Here are the key points from this chapter that will help you to develop and apply your ROI mindset.

- An ROI mindset helps you to prioritize actions and decisions that are most likely to generate meaningful value in return for your effort.

- Like all salespeople, you work with finite and often costly resources – especially your time. So how and where you invest these matters greatly.

- Understanding the true cost of your sales efforts will help you to evaluate whether your investment is worthwhile, or whether you're better off investing elsewhere.

- A cost only becomes an investment when it's aimed at producing a return, and returns aren't always guaranteed. So assessing likelihood and risk is vital.

- ROI isn't always just financial. Intangible benefits such as learning from failed sales or gaining case studies can still contribute to long-term success.

- To maximize your ROI, focus on improving your sales efficiency, effectiveness, consistency and volume, rather than trying to over-optimize one single area.

Chapter 6
How can you get
a little better?

The growth mindset

In the previous chapter we explored the ROI mindset, which is built on the principle that you should continually seek to improve your return on investment. The growth mindset is similar but different, because it involves continually seeking to improve your abilities in *all* areas.

The growth mindset is a belief that it's always possible to improve your abilities and intelligence through effort. So it's a mindset that's as applicable to building on strengths as it is to overcoming challenges and setbacks. It is, to paraphrase a famous quote from Thomas Edison, the belief that there's *always* a way to do it better – you just have to find it.

So applying a growth mindset to sales involves believing that there's *always* something you can do to improve your sales performance.

The key elements of sales performance

Your sales performance is the result of your sales efficiency, effectiveness, consistency and volume.

If you wrote this as a formula (which I won't, because after the chapter on ROI you've probably had enough of calculations for a while), it would be each element multiplied by the next rather than the four elements added together. The reason for this is that any small improvements you make across these areas tend to compound up to deliver a much bigger result overall.

So think of your sales efficiency, effectiveness, consistency and volume, as four separate levers that you can pull to generate a better overall result.

I'll give you some examples of how you can improve each of these areas shortly, but first I want to show you why improving them, even by a small amount, can have a huge impact on your total sales performance.

Harnessing the power of marginal gains

As I've explained previously, in sales there are no sure-fire ways to guarantee success. But you can take lots of small actions, which, when added together, will greatly improve your probability of achieving the objective you're working towards.

The same is true in almost any field of human endeavour. So to help explain the power of aggregating marginal gains, here's a story from the world of sport.

When Sir David Brailsford became performance director of British Cycling, he set about breaking down the objective of winning races into its component parts. He believed that if he could make just a 1% improvement in a host of different areas, the cumulative effect would be hugely significant. But what made him different is that he took this concept to the extreme.

Here are some examples of the small improvements he made.

> He knew that each time a team member got ill, even if it was just a minor cold, their performance suffered. He also knew that most infections are spread through poor hand hygiene – so he taught the whole team how to wash their hands properly to help reduce the likelihood of illness.

> By analysing the mechanics area in the team truck he discovered that dust was accumulating on the floor, which he reasoned was probably finding its way into the bikes' bearings and undermining their performance. So he had the floor of the truck painted white, which showed when and where dirt was building up, increasing the probability it would be kept clean.

▶ He knew that a good night's sleep is the most important factor for recovery, but that it wasn't always easy for his team to achieve as they travelled around the world, moving from hotel to hotel. So he created the 'bed in the bag' system where a rider's mattress, pillow and bedding travel with them – meaning they effectively got to sleep in their own bed every night, increasing the chance that they'll feel rested and rejuvenated the next day.

These are just a few examples as he tried hundreds of ways to make small changes that would each result in a marginal performance gain, because he believed that the overall impact would be much greater than the sum of its parts.

To say this was a successful approach is an understatement. Great Britain used to be an 'also-ran' in the world of cycling, but Team GB led the cycling medal table at both of the next Olympic Games, winning eight gold medals at each, and British cyclists went on to win 59 World Championships over the next ten years.

You'd now be hard pressed to find a professional sports team anywhere in the world, or an elite performer in any industry, who doesn't actively harness the power of marginal gains.

How to apply this approach

To apply this approach you need to utilize your growth mindset, and focus on the belief that there's *always* a way to do it better – you just have to find it.

But it's better to focus on doing 100 things 1% better, than it is to try to do one thing 100% better. So make one small change you believe will help, and then see if it has a positive or negative impact before you add more. This is because if you make lots of changes in one area at once, you won't know which ones are helping and which ones aren't.

But be careful not to make up your mind too quickly. Mastering more complex sales skills is like learning a new language – you're likely to make a lot of mistakes before you get it right. So in some cases, things that don't appear to work first time are worth sticking with for a while before you make a decision about whether they're helping or not.

Make one small change, reflect on what happened, ditch the change if it had a negative impact, but keep it if it improved your performance. Then make another change, and keep repeating the process.

Why this approach works

This approach works because not only is it easier to continually make lots of small adjustments rather than one big change, but because making lots of small adjustments one after the other also triggers a compounding or snowball effect.

If you were to roll a snowball down a hill, and each time it rotated it grew in size by 1%, then it would continually get both larger and faster, because each time it went around it would grow by 1% of a bigger snowball.

Exactly the same thing happens when you make lots of small improvement cycles one after another. If you could find a way to improve your performance by 1% each day, after a year you wouldn't be 365% better, you'd actually have improved by 3,678%, due to the compounding effect. Of course, a 1% improvement every day isn't realistic. But even improving by 1% a week can have a significant impact over time.

Sales performance improvement examples

Here are some examples of how the marginal gains approach can be applied to different sales situations to drive a significant performance improvement.

The Drinkit sales team

In the previous chapter I shared a worked example of a Drinkit salesperson who spent 220 days selling each year, visiting an average of 12 prospective customers a day, with an average win-rate of 8.4%.

Let's look at what would happen to those key performance indicators if they made just a small marginal gain in each of those three areas.

- ▶ If they worked on improving their efficiency to give them 1% more selling time, perhaps by reducing the amount of time they spend on non-productive tasks, that would give them two more selling days each year.

- ▶ If they also worked on improving the volume of prospective customers they visited each day by 1%, perhaps through better journey planning, that would result in them making 51 more visits each year. This would be a 2% increase in their number of visits, because the benefit of the improved journey planning would compound on top of the additional selling days.

▶ If they also worked on their effectiveness and improved their sales conversion rate by 1%, perhaps by using any of the sales skills I'll explain in Part 3, that would result in them closing 31 more sales each year. This would be a 14% increase in their number of sales, again partly due to the compounding effect of the improvements they'd made to their selling time and visit rate.

So making just three marginal gains would result in a huge improvement to their overall sales performance.

The SupportIT sales team

Each member of the SupportIT sales team is currently closing one sale per day, on average.

If they could find a way to consistently improve their performance by just 1% each week, by the end of a year, instead of making five sales a week they'd be making more than eight, which would be a 68% increase.

Maybe you think that a 1% improvement every week is a little ambitious? Even if they improved their sales performance by just 0.5% each week, by the end of the year that would still mean they'd be averaging 6.5 sales each week, which would still be a 30% increase.

Either way, these results would represent a significant improvement to their sales performance, simply driven by a consistently applied series of marginal gains.

If you'd like to watch a short video showing just how those marginal gains stack up over time for the SupportIT sales team, or download a tool so you can model how small improvements could impact your own sales results, you can access both for free at greatersales.com/bookextras.

Chapter 6: Summary

The growth mindset is the belief that your abilities and intelligence can always be improved through effort, which means there's always a way to do it better.

Here are the key points from this chapter about how to apply a growth mindset to your sales activities to improve your overall performance.

▶ Your sales performance is driven by four key factors: efficiency, effectiveness, consistency and volume.

▷ Even small improvements in these areas can compound over time to deliver big results.

▷ The marginal gains approach is about making lots of small manageable changes that build momentum.

▷ Success comes from trying one change at a time, tracking the impact, and continuing to build on what works.

▷ There are countless examples from the worlds of sport and sales that show how powerful this approach can be when applied consistently.

Part 1: Conclusion

Continually applying the six essential mindsets we've covered in Part 1 will help you to keep improving as you move through this book and your sales career.

So before you move on to Part 2, take a moment to reflect on each of these. How will applying the win-win mindset, the trust-builder mindset, the value-add mindset, the decision-focused mindset, the ROI mindset and the growth mindset, help you to drive your sales performance?

In Part 2 you're going to build on these mindsets as I show you everything you need to know – the five essential areas of knowledge that all salespeople need to develop. Then in Part 3, I'm going to show you how to put your sales mindsets and knowledge into action – explaining exactly what you need to do to have efficient, effective and consistently good sales conversations that deliver high volumes of results. So there's lots to come.

Before I do that though, I also want you to reflect on something I shared with you in the introduction. Right back at the start of this book, I said that if you hit a chapter that feels daunting, don't worry. Just identify one thing you can put into action that you think will make a positive difference, focus on doing that, and make a note to come back to the chapter again later. *That's* the growth mindset and the marginal gains principle in action.

Continue to focus on that as you move forward. Don't be afraid to build at your own pace, but ensure you keep coming back to drive further improvements as you grow.

PART 2

WHAT YOU NEED TO KNOW: THE FIVE ESSENTIAL AREAS OF KNOWLEDGE FOR GREATER SALESPEOPLE

Chapter 7
What you're selling

In Part 1 I introduced you to the idea that selling is the process of helping someone to make an informed buying decision by exploring and targeting a win-win outcome. But while that alludes to *how* you should sell, it doesn't explain *what* you're selling.

The answer might seem obvious, but this is an area where most salespeople can benefit from developing or refreshing their knowledge, because having a deep understanding of what you're selling will help hugely when you come to put your knowledge into action.

Why you're always selling ideas

If you ask salespeople what they sell, most will describe the products or services that their company makes or supplies, some may talk about selling solutions to their customers' problems, but very few will say that they sell ideas. In reality, before you can sell a product or service, or get to the point where you start to solve your customer's problems, you have to sell the customer on the *idea of change*.

In his 2018 book, *Gap Selling*, Keenan focuses in on this idea, where the 'gap' he refers to is the space between a prospect's current state and their desired future state, or 'where they want to be'. Gap selling is then about positioning your solution as the change that fills or bridges that gap. Not only is this approach completely compatible with the New 7-Step Sales process you'll learn in Part 3, but its one that the process actively promotes, as you shouldn't move on to propose and present a solution (Step 4), before you've truly understood where your customer wants to get to (which is Step 3).

Before you get to that stage of your sales conversation, you've got to sell the customer on the idea of changing what they're doing *right now*.

In most cases, when you're selling to a prospective customer, the first thing you're doing is interrupting them. Even when a customer proactively approaches a salesperson, they're usually only doing so either to get information they couldn't quickly or easily find elsewhere, or they're just looking for the salesperson to facilitate the transaction. So in most cases, the first thing you'll need to do is sell the customer on the *idea* that they should give you some of their valuable time, or possibly just more of their time than they were expecting. Of course that's even more true when you're cold-calling prospective customers who weren't expecting to hear from you at all.

But even once a customer is sold on the idea of having a conversation with you, that doesn't mean they're yet sold on the idea of changing what they're doing, or on the idea of buying from you or your organization.

This is an idea we've explored before. In Part 1 you learnt about the status quo bias, which is a type of automatic risk-averse thinking we all have. Everyone's brain is wired to prefer the current situation, so all customers will be resistant to change to some degree, even those who proactively approach a salesperson.

Overcoming resistance to change is also something we're going to come back to. In Part 3 I'll show you how selling the idea of change can be embedded into every step of your sales conversation, including how to handle and overcome objections if a customer actively voices their resistance to the change you're proposing.

But for now, I just want you to recognize that sales is about selling the idea of change, as much as it is about selling products or services.

Why you've got to sell a package

'A rose by any other name would smell as sweet.' This quote from Shakespeare's *Romeo and Juliet* helps to shed a little light on how we all see the world. It suggests that a name is just a label we use to distinguish one type of thing from another, and doesn't hold much value or worth in itself.

As humans, one way that we understand and can explain the world is by categorizing similar things into groups that we then name. But on its own, the name we use for a group of similar things doesn't really have much value or meaning. For example, if I told you I own 'a house', that wouldn't give you enough detail to picture it. Or if I offered to sell you 'a car' for £5,000, you wouldn't know whether that was good value or not without a lot more information.

As we explored in Part 1, it's the features of a product or service that give it value. There I explained that features are things that a product or service *has, is, does* or *comes with*. While the value of a feature might be subjective, features are factual. They're things that everyone would agree exist, or that most people would objectively agree are true.

So for our Drinkit team, the features of their pale ale might include information about its taste profile, visual appeal, alcohol level, typical sales volumes or margin, its uniqueness, its competitive position, and the marketing support it comes with for their business customers, and so on.

For example, Drinkit Pale Ale is:

▶ brewed from just four ingredients: water, malt, yeast and hops;

▶ alcohol free;

▶ clear, with a pale golden colour and a white head;

▶ gluten free;

▶ caffeine free;

▶ suitable for vegans;

▶ low in calories;

▶ available in 330ml bottles, 440ml cans or 20-litre draught kegs; and

▶ is the number one draught non-alcoholic beer sold in free-trade pubs and bars.

As long as it's something that most people would objectively agree on, and is proven to be true, or complies with an accepted set of standards, then features can also be things that a product does. So you could say that the features of Drinkit Pale Ale are also that it:

▶ provides a crisp and refreshing taste;

▶ produces a mild calming effect that's similar to drinking small quantities of alcohol; and

▶ typically delivers 12% more profit than the leading non-alcoholic beer sold in supermarkets.

A feature can also be something that a product or service comes with. So when it's being sold to a pub or a bar, the features that Drinkit Pale Ale comes with could include:

▶ a free 20-litre keg for new customers;

▶ free branded glassware, beer mats and bar runners;

▶ free table-top point-of-sale material;

▶ a free staff or customer tasting session run by the Drinkit sales rep;

▶ access to the Drinkit customer loyalty programme; and

▶ sales and technical support provided by the Drinkit team throughout the year.

As you can see, the Drinkit sales team never just sell beer, they sell a package that's made up of multiple features.

The same is true for you and your customers. You never just sell a product or a service, and that's not what your customers buy either. It's always a package deal.

Activity: Know your features

Make a short list of the core products or services that you sell. For each one, list the features that it *has, is, does, comes with*, or *could come with*.

List as many features as you can think of. Don't worry about how relevant you think they are at this stage. You'll be coming back to this list and refining further, later in this chapter. Make sure though, that you only include features you're confident are factually correct or objectively true.

Selling advantages and benefits

In Chapter 3 I introduced you to the FAB cycle and the four elements it contains – needs, features, advantages and benefits. There I explained that customers will only buy things they believe are going to benefit them, which is why the basic premise behind producing and selling products and services is as follows.

1. It's possible to identify groups of customers with similar **needs**.

2. When that happens, organizations design products or services that include *features* that satisfy those needs. Innovative companies also create features that customers didn't know they needed or wanted until they knew about them, which is why the arrow between needs and features in Figure 3 – the FAB cycle – points both ways.

3. The *advantages* of those features can be understood by anyone, but…

4. … they only *benefit* an individual customer if they satisfy the customer's *personal* needs or wants.

This principle of selling someone not only on the features and advantages of your package, but also on how they'll personally benefit from them is important, and it's something that we're going to come back to in Part 3. But the most efficient and effective sales conversations are those based on a deep knowledge and understanding of what you're selling, so let's continue to build that first.

Activity: Understanding advantages and benefits

Step 1: Know your advantages
Pull out the list of features you created in the last activity. Alongside each one, briefly describe the advantage that feature provides. Remember that advantages need to be understood by anyone, so at this stage the description for each advantage needs to be relatively generic.

One tip for helping you to describe the advantage of each feature is to try to imagine a typical customer saying: 'I care about [this feature], *because* of [it's advantage]'.

For example, Drinkit's pub-owning customers might say:

▶ 'I care about stocking an alcohol-free beer, because I need products that appeal to drivers'; or

▶ 'I care about receiving free glassware, because it saves me money over buying my own'; or

▶ 'I care about stocking products with a high rate of sale, because higher sales equals higher profits'.

Step 2: Understand the potential benefits

Unlike your more widely relatable advantages, benefits are personal, so it's not possible to explain how every feature and advantage will benefit every prospective customer, because it won't.

I'm going to show you how to understand and sell the benefits of your product or service to each customer in a personalized way in Part 3. But I don't want to leave you hanging until then, so let's continue the activity to develop your understanding about where we're heading by exploring the level of benefit that each of your features potentially provides.

On the list you've created, put a number that represents how interested or excited your prospective customers typically are about each feature and advantage pair.

▶ If it's something they don't care about, score it zero.

▶ If it's something they might care about but don't ask about, score it 1.

▶ If it's something a typical prospect is actively interested in, score it 2.

▶ If it's something most prospects are very interested in or even excited about, score it 3.

You've now got a list that you can rank in priority order, from high-scoring features that are probably going to be important for you to focus on, versus low-scoring features that aren't.

You can also use these scores to map your features back to the values needs and wants lens I introduced in Chapter 3.

▶ Any feature with a score of 3 represents something that most customers actively want.

▶ Any feature with a score of 2 represents something that satisfies a customer's motivational need.

▶ Any feature with a score of 1 represents something that most customers would silently expect any relevant product or service to include.

▶ And any feature with a score of 0 is a feature that probably doesn't satisfy any meaningful need or want at all!

Those features with a score of 2 or 3, and the advantages and benefits they provide, represent your *value proposition*. Collectively they explain why a customer might choose that product or service over another – because of the *value* it provides.

Keep hold of the list you've created. Not only will you find it helpful when you get to Part 3, but it'll also be useful for you to refer back to during the next chapter, as we explore what type of customers you need to target.

Chapter 7: Summary

Selling is more than just showcasing your product or service. It's about helping your customer to recognize and believe in the value of change. The most effective salespeople understand what they're really selling and how to position it in a way that resonates with their customers' needs and wants.

Here are the key points from this chapter.

- You're not just selling products or services; you're also selling the idea of change.

- Every sale starts with selling the customer on the idea of giving you some of their time and attention.

- What you sell is always a package made up of multiple features – things your product or service *has, is, does,* or *comes with*.

- Features provide advantages that anyone can understand, but personalized benefits motivate customers to buy.

- Your value proposition is built around the features that most closely align with your customers' motivational needs and emotional wants.

Chapter 8
Who to target

An organization's market can be defined as the group of customers (including prospective, active and lapsed customers) who may benefit from the products or services it sells. It's a big group made up of lots of different people or businesses who, at least in theory, would find their products or services useful.

For example, SupportIT's market could include anyone who owns or uses IT equipment; Drinkit's market could include any business that could sell beer, plus any person who could buy beer for themselves or for other people in their household; and the Widget Store's market could include anyone who might need or want any of the thousands of widgets it stocks.

These are very large groups of customers, and so most companies tend to specialize and narrow their focus.

Understanding your target market

Your target market is the group of customers to whom your products or services are *specifically* tailored and aimed. It's a group of customers who are likely to get significant benefit from what you're selling, and are therefore more likely to buy from you.

If you think about the companies where our salespeople work, the Widget Store would describe their target market as consumers who value quality and experience over price, SupportIT would describe their target market as small businesses, and Drinkit would describe their target market as independent pubs and licensed retailers (and indirectly also their consumers, who may be looking to moderate or abstain from drinking alcohol for different reasons).

But in each case, these target markets still contain a lot of potentially very different customers. So salespeople, and marketers, can benefit from narrowing their focus even further by splitting their target market into smaller segments, with each segment being a sub-group of customers who are all very similar.

The benefit of segmenting your target market into small groups is that it helps you to tailor your approach and improve your chances of success. Each group is different from the others because it contains customers who are all very similar, and are all likely to benefit from a specific product or service you sell for the same reasons. Understanding how to segment your target market, and then target different groups of customers with different offers and messages, significantly increases your chances of opening conversations and closing sales. Let's look at some examples of how this can work with our three different sales teams.

The SupportIT sales team targets small businesses who work with confidential customer data and have between five and 50 employees. They do this because businesses who care about customer confidentiality readily recognize the benefits of protecting their devices and the data they hold, but are probably not yet big enough to have their own IT team to help them do that in-house. They also target family-run or owner-managed businesses, because they find their decision-makers often work long hours and so recognize the benefits of having IT support available 24/7. But they don't target businesses with fewer than five staff, because in these cases they tend to find their onboarding fees are often a financial barrier for the customer.

The Drinkit off-trade team targets independent licensed retailers who operate between one and five stores. They only target licensed retailers, because even though Drinkit beer is non-alcoholic and so *could* be sold without a premises licence, they find non-licensed stores don't deliver the rate of sale they want to achieve. As a field sales team, they also target independently owned businesses with small numbers of stores to maximize the chances that they'll be able to meet with a decision-maker when they visit, leaving larger groups of centrally managed stores to be targeted by Drinkit's national accounts team. They especially like to target retailers who buy from one of Drinkit's platinum wholesale partners as those wholesalers offer great deals, which enables their retail customers to sell Drinkit beer at very competitive prices, and so they tend to deliver higher rates of sale.

The Widget sales team is different. As a store-based sales team they can only sell to walk-in customers, and so it's the marketing team's role to identify and reach out to the right customer segments, and to encourage high-potential customers to visit the store. Once customers are in store, the Widget sales team uses a process of customer qualification to prioritize which customers they're going to target their time and energy towards. You'll learn more about qualifying customers when we explore their role in the sales pipeline in Chapter 10.

A note on target markets vs ideal customer profiles

In addition to target markets, another term that's commonly used in sales is *ideal customer profile* (or ICP). As we've just covered, your target market refers to the group of customers to whom your products or services are specifically tailored and aimed. In contrast, your ICP is a more specific and detailed description of your perfect customer – someone who would benefit most from your product or service and be most valuable to you in return.

So the two terms are similar but slightly different. Think of your target market as the ocean you're fishing in, and your ideal customer profile as the exact type of fish you're trying to catch. You fish in the target market, and you target a specific type of fish that lives within it.

Activity: Understand your target market and ICPs

In no more than three sentences, broadly describe your target market.

Then, define two or three different segments of customers within it. Each segment should define a group of customers who are similar to each other, but who are different from those in your other segments. Focus on defining groups of customers who are both likely to buy from you *and* could deliver a volume of sales that would make your efforts worthwhile. It's no good identifying a gap in the market if there's not a big enough market in the gap!

For inspiration, take time to look over your sales records.

When defining your target market, are there some similarities that the majority of your good customers share? If so, why do you think that's the case? Look back over the list of features, advantages and potential benefits you created in the previous chapter too. What type of customer would those appeal to most strongly?

If you then had to split your good customers into a few smaller groups, how would you do that? What makes the customers in one group different from those in another? Now choose or imagine a customer that typifies each group. Those are your ideal customers. So a description of each one is *one* of your ideal customer profiles. Targeting customers who look like one of your ICPs is usually a good way to improve your sales efficiency and effectiveness.

Targeting competitors

It's important that you understand your competitors, but you shouldn't directly target them. You might, however, target their customers, *if* you can identify that you have a competitive advantage that could make your products or services a better fit.

For example, the SupportIT sales team might target customers of competitors who don't offer 24/7 support, specifically those with business hours beyond the typical nine-to-five day, where their always-available IT support could be a competitive advantage. The Drinkit on-trade sales team might target pubs that stock beer from one of their competitors that only offers non-alcoholic beer in bottles or cans – where their ability to provide Drinkit beer on tap could be a competitive advantage.

The key is that in both cases the sales teams are not targeting their competitors; they're targeting a specific competitor's customers for specific reasons – customers for whom they believe their products or services would provide greater *value*.

Talking about your competitors

While it's obvious that you should avoid negative words when describing your own products and services, you should also avoid speaking negatively about your competitors. After all, would you believe a salesperson's scathing opinion of one of their rivals? Possibly, although probably not. Even if you thought what they were saying had an element of truth, you know their opinion is inherently biased – so you'd probably doubt whether they were giving you the full picture.

When it comes to your competitors, the best approach is usually not to mention them at all unless your customer does so first. But if they do, stick to making brief factual statements about your competitor that are neither positive nor negative, then emphasize how your products or services are *different*, and why your customer should care. Try using phrases like this:

> '*[That competitor] does [this], whereas we do [this], which we feel is better for our customers, because...*'

Sticking to this approach will help to ensure you're seen as a professional, ethical and trustworthy salesperson, because, as you learnt in Part 1, when it comes to sales, gaining and maintaining your customer's trust is incredibly important.

Activity: Understand where you have a competitive advantage

You're unlikely to be in a situation where every prospective customer would agree that your products or services are better than those from all of your competitors. However, there are probably specific types of customer who are more likely to see the features and advantages of your offer as being more beneficial, and a better fit for their needs.

Understanding the types of customer where you have a true competitive advantage can help you to target your sales activities more effectively, and lead to sales conversations that are more efficient and effective as a result. This activity will help you to do that.

Make a list of your significant direct competitors – those who offer products and services that customers would say are similar to yours.

Then, for each competitor, look over the target market segments you identified in the last activity. For each one consider why a customer from that segment might get more value buying from you rather than from that competitor. The features and advantages lists you created previously should help. You should consider factors such as these.

- ▶ **Product and service range.** Do you offer products or services that this competitor doesn't? How wide is your range of options compared to theirs?

- ▶ **Unique Selling Points (or USPs).** Are there any significant features that your products or services have that theirs don't?

▶ **Price.** Are your prices more competitive? Or are your payment terms more attractive?

▶ **Quality.** Are your products or services objectively higher quality than theirs? Do you have any quality marks, awards or customer reviews that help to prove that?

▶ **Customer service.** Do you offer better customer service? Again, do you have any awards, testimonials or customer reviews that could help to demonstrate that?

▶ **Support.** Do you offer better support for customers after they've purchased from you, perhaps by providing support that's easier because it's available through more channels? Or do you offer more marketing support to drive consumer recognition, and help your B2B customers to sell-on your products or services more effectively?

▶ **Location.** Is your location or coverage better suited to customers in some areas than your competitor's?

This activity will help you to identify the segments of your target market where you have a particular advantage over some, if not all, of your competitors. It can also help you to start creating competitor battlecards.

A competitor battlecard is a short document no more than one page of quick and easy-to-read tables or bullet-points. This note-style information can help you when you're battling to win a customer's business over a specific competitor. Rather than including details about all of your features and advantages, they focus on the key differences between your offering and that of your competitor, highlight your USPs and suggest how you could describe the differences between yours and your competitor's products to show why your solution is a better fit.

If your organization doesn't use competitor battlecards and you think they might be useful, reach out to your sales leadership and marketing team to ask about creating some.

Chapter 8: Summary

Understanding who to target is a vital part of sales success. By narrowing your focus and tailoring your approach, you significantly improve your chances of making meaningful connections and closing more sales.

Here are the key points we covered in this chapter.

▶ *Target markets* are the groups of customers your products or services are specifically aimed at. These groups are often broad and varied.

▶ *Segmenting your target* market into smaller and more tightly defined customer groups allows you to personalize your approach and improve your success rate.

▶ *Ideal customer profiles (ICPs)* describe the perfect customer within a worthwhile segment – those most likely to benefit from what you sell and deliver the most value to you in return.

▶ Identifying where you have an edge over your competitors can also help you to focus your efforts where they're likely to deliver the greatest return.

▶ Speaking professionally about competitors builds trust – so avoid criticizing them. Instead, highlight the important ways your offer is different, and therefore probably more valuable to the customer.

Chapter 9
Your goals, objectives, targets and KPIs

… because if you don't know where you're heading and how you intend to get there, you'll probably end up somewhere else.

What you need to know

The terms *goals*, *objectives* and *targets* are often used interchangeably. For example, you may hear phrases such as 'our goals are stretching but entirely achievable', 'this year's objectives are especially challenging', or 'we've set ambitious targets for this quarter', and you could probably swap these three terms around in those phrases and for most people the meaning wouldn't change. However, goals, objectives and targets are not the same, and it's important to know the difference.

Goal: a broad or long-term definition of success. Goals are direction-setting statements that broadly describe what success looks like at a point in the medium to long-term future. A company should use its goals to help define its strategy, which then describes *how* the company will achieve its goals. For example, a company might have a goal to achieve a certain level of profit, but they might be able to achieve that through a strategy that focuses on increasing sales volumes, or by focusing on selling more profitable products or services without necessarily increasing their top-line sales figure.

Objectives: specific, measurable milestones on route to the goal. Objectives define specific actions you'll take to work towards your goal, and each one represents a milestone to achieve along the way. For example, if your company's overall goal is to become the market leader, one objective to help achieve that might be to start selling to a new market segment. However, to be truly effective, each objective should be SMART, which stands for Specific, Measurable, Achievable, Relevant (in that it's linked to the company's goal) and Time-bound.

I like to add an extra 'A' to the SMART acronym so it becomes SMAART. This is because it's important for objectives to be *Aspirational* as well as *Achievable*. Objectives that are easy to achieve without even trying don't motivate people at all. But objectives that are so aspirational they're unlikely ever to be met can actively demotivate. It's important to get the balance right.

Figure 4: The SMAART objective system

Target: a short-term numeric aim that quantifies an objective. Targets are typically defined by a definitive number. They're often incorporated into objectives because they help to make the objective more specific, enable progress against the objective to be measured, and ensure it's clear when the objective has been met. For example, if your company's goal is to become the market leader and one objective to help it get there is to sell more to existing customers, your target might be to grow the overall value of existing customer accounts by 10% by the end of this year.

KPI: a key performance indicator that helps to measure progress. Key performance indicators (or KPIs) are measurable metrics that tell you what's happening or what happened in the past. This makes them different from *goals*, *objectives* and *targets*, because they're all forward looking. Well-chosen KPIs can help to explain why a company, team or individual's performance is what it is. If you're ahead or behind on your journey to achieve your objective and hit your target, your KPIs should help to explain why, and should also indicate what you could do to improve.

As I explained when we looked at your performance drivers in Figure 1, sales KPIs can be split into two types: input KPIs and output KPIs. Input KPIs measure those things that are within your direct control like your call rate, and so they sit within your pyramid. Output KPIs measure things that you can influence but that are outside of your direct control, like the number of sales you make, and so they sit outside of your pyramid, directly below your sales objective.

| INPUT KPIs | OUTPUT KPIs | TARGET | OBJECTIVE | GOAL |

Figure 5: KPIs, targets, objectives and goals

In short, and as Figure 5 illustrates, KPIs feed into achieving targets, which roll up into objectives, which fulfil a goal.

Setting effective sales goals, objectives, targets and KPIs is a real skill. Get them right, and they can help bond and motivate a team and drive the right behaviours. Get them wrong, and they can have exactly the opposite effect. This is why, for most salespeople, these are set for them by their company or sales leadership team.

What you need to understand

It's not only important for you to know what your goals, objectives, targets and KPIs are, but you also need to understand how they all fit together.

We explored the ROI mindset in Part 1, and one of the principles of that is to invest heavily in the activities that directly contribute towards your objectives, and to streamline or eliminate those that don't.

So understanding how your sales activities are linked to your goals, objectives, targets and KPIs is important, because any activity you invest significant time, energy or resources into, should contribute towards all of these. If you don't understand how it does then you should question whether it's the right thing to do, as ideally you want to streamline or eliminate those activities that don't help to generate a meaningful return.

But if you're questioning others rather than yourself, especially those in your sales leadership team, then you need to do so sensitively. It may well be that there's a link between the activity and your objective that you don't yet understand, or that you're being asked to do something that helps another part of the business contribute towards your shared goal in a way you hadn't previously recognized.

Activity: Understanding your goals, objectives, targets and KPIs

If you don't already know what your organization's goal is, take time to find out. Not all organizations have one written down, so don't be surprised if yours doesn't. But if not, then it's definitely worth asking someone from your leadership team about how they would describe it.

Most sales teams, however, have clear objectives and targets. Some will have more than one. For example, they may have an objective that's ten years or so into the future, with annual targets for each year leading up to it. But *all* sales teams should have objectives or targets for the current year. If you don't know what your teams' are, then find out.

Every salesperson should also have a clear personal objective or target too. The most common of these, and I believe the most useful, are *annual targets*. For me, an annual target hits that sweet spot. That's because it's far enough away to allow time to monitor your performance and take any necessary corrective actions, but not so far away that it becomes something you can afford to forget about for now. Make sure you know what your annual target is. If one hasn't been set for you, now's the time to create one for yourself.

Finally, consider what your KPIs are. Again, these might be set and measured for you. If they're not, decide which sales behaviours and outcomes you can measure for yourself that could indicate how you're performing and potentially highlight areas where you could improve.

Once you've collected this information, write it down as a hierarchical list.

- ▶ At the top of the page, write down your organization's long-term goal.

- ▶ Below it, write your team's longer-term objective or target. If you have a series of targets for different years, for example, write them down in sequence, starting with the furthest away at the top, working down to the most imminent at the bottom.

▸ Below your *team's* objectives or targets, write down *your* personal short-term or annual target.

▸ Then below your target, list your KPIs – the things you're going to specifically measure that indicate how you're performing. If you know which are your inputs and which are your outputs, then write the output KPIs first with your input KPIs beneath them. If you're not sure which are which, or if you can't split them that way, then write them side-by-side across the page.

Finally, draw an upward arrow to connect each element of your list to the one above it; an arrow pointing from your KPIs up to your target; an arrow from your target up to your team's objective; and an arrow from your team's objective up to your organization's long-term goal.

These arrows show how your sales activities that impact your KPIs not only help you to achieve *your* target, but also directly help both your team and your organization to get where it wants to go. Understanding this can be a powerful motivator. It can also help you to frame how you describe your own actions and intentions when speaking with your sales manager or members of your company's leadership team.

A worked example

Here's an example of what the results of that activity might look like for a member of the Drinkit on-trade team. It shows how their KPIs, target and objective all link together to help the company achieve its overall goal.

Long-term company goal: For Drinkit to be the market leader for non-alcoholic beer, within five years.

↑

On-trade sales team objective: To sell 30 million litres of Drinkit beer through independent pubs and bars, during this financial year.

↑

Individual sales target: For each salesperson to develop and maintain a minimum of 650 Drinkit beer stockists in their territory by the end of the financial year, each selling a minimum of 1.5 kegs per week. (For context, this target represents a *net* growth of 165 new stockists per person, requiring the sales team to focus on both winning new customers *and* on retaining existing customer accounts.)

↑

Output KPIs: The number of draught beer customers in the salesperson's territory at the start of the year, plus the number of new customers won, and the number of customers lost, giving the total number of currently active customer accounts.

↑

Input KPIs: The number of customers visited by the salesperson each week, split into the number of prospective customers versus existing customer accounts.

Chapter 9: Summary

Knowing the difference between your goals, objectives, targets and KPIs – and how they all connect – is essential if you want to stay focused, make better decisions and deliver meaningful results.

Here are the key points to take away from this chapter.

- ▶ Goals describe your long-term ambition and broadly describe what success looks like in the future.

- ▷ Objectives break that ambition down into clear, measurable milestones, and should be SMAART – which means Specific, Measurable, Aspirational, Achievable, Relevant and Time-bound.

- ▶ Targets quantify your objectives and help you to measure whether they've been met, usually by defining a clear number and timeframe.

- ▷ KPIs track progress and performance – they show what's happening and help you to understand why things are going well or where improvement is needed.

- ▷ Input KPIs measure the actions you take and are within your control., Output KPIs reflect the outcomes you can influence but can't fully control.

▶ Everything should link together. Your KPIs should help you hit your target, your target should drive your objective, and your objective should move you closer to your goal.

This structure should help to guide your thinking and actions – if something isn't contributing to the chain, it's worth questioning whether it needs to be done at all.

Chapter 10
Your role in the sales pipeline

What is a sales pipeline?

A sales pipeline is an organized and visual way of defining the stages a customer moves through from a salesperson's perspective. An organization's sales pipeline should start with potential or future customers at the top, moving down through different stages, until you reach lapsed customers at the bottom.

A sales pipeline is similar, but not identical, to a sales process. A *sales pipeline* refers to the stages that customers move through, whereas a *sales process* refers to the actions you take to move a customer from one stage of the pipeline to the next.

We'll cover sales pipelines in this chapter. In the next chapter I'll show you why a sales pipeline is also useful when it comes to creating sales strategies and plans. Then, in Part 3, you'll learn all about the New 7-Step Sales process, and how to use it to drive customers through your pipeline as you put your strategies and plans into action.

One of the benefits of a defined sales pipeline is that it can help you to understand how all of these different elements are aligned: your customers, your strategies and plans, and your sales activities.

As you can see from Figure 6, your sales pipeline starts at the top with your *suspects*. These are the people or businesses who you *suspect* you might be able to help. As a salesperson, your role might include finding, investigating and pre-qualifying these suspects.

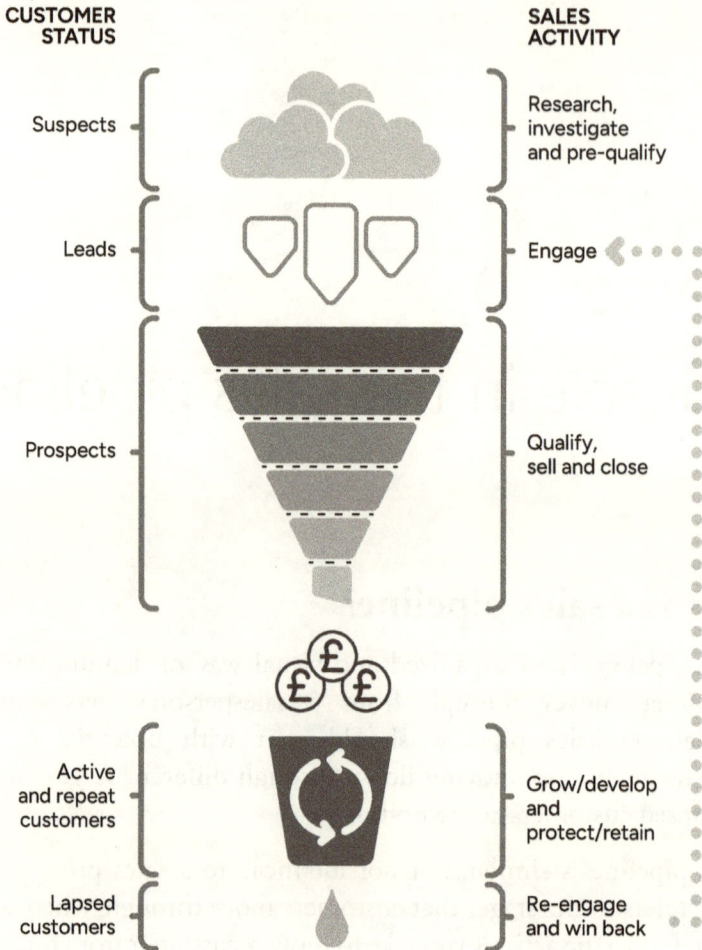

CUSTOMER STATUS

Suspects

Leads

Prospects

Active and repeat customers

Lapsed customers

SALES ACTIVITY

Research, investigate and pre-qualify

Engage

Qualify, sell and close

Grow/develop and protect/retain

Re-engage and win back

Figure 6: The funnel, sieve and bucket sales pipeline model

Sales qualification is the process of evaluating how likely it is that a customer might buy what you're selling. Qualifying, or disqualifying, customers is an important process because if there's something that makes them unlikely to buy from you, or perhaps unable to buy from you even if they wanted to, the earlier you can identify that the better. From the moment you start to engage with a customer, you'll continue to evaluate and qualify them all the way through your pipeline. Your pre-qualification actions at the very top are just the beginning.

Moving down your pipeline, the next level beneath your suspects are your *leads*. Leads are the people or businesses where you've identified something specific about them that *leads* you to believe you could help. As a salesperson, your role will probably include engaging leads in conversation. As you do, you'll continue to qualify whether they're someone who you can and would like to help, just as they'll start to qualify whether you're someone they want to engage with too.

Once you've successfully engaged a lead and opened a conversation, they move down to the next stage of your sales pipeline, where your prospects sit. *Prospects*, or prospective customers, are the people or businesses with whom you're actively engaged in conversation. As a salesperson, your role will likely be to sell to these prospects, and close sales with them, in order to turn them into customers.

In the sales pipeline diagram, your prospects sit within your sales funnel. This funnel is wide at the top to represent lots of prospects at the initial engagement stage, and narrower at the bottom because the funnel contains a number of sieves. These sieves represent the continual qualification process that happens from both sides. For example, during your conversation you might discover something that makes your prospect a bad fit for you. Maybe you discover they're not big enough to meet your minimum order requirement, so you might disqualify them, politely end the conversation for now, and schedule to check back in with them again in future. Or they might discover something that makes you a bad fit for them, disqualifying you and removing themselves from the conversation, politely or not, as a result. Or, if you don't do a good enough job of keeping your prospect engaged, they might become disengaged and just wander off, perhaps to go and talk to one of your competitors instead.

Hopefully you're not going to lose prospects because they become passively disengaged, but no matter how good a salesperson you are, the number of prospects that reach the lower stages of your pipeline will be less than the number of leads you successfully engaged higher up. So your funnel may narrow sharply if you lose a lot, or may be steeper-sided if you do a great job at pre-qualifying your suspects and keeping your prospects actively engaged. But no salesperson successfully closes every sale, so this section of your pipeline is always going to be funnel-shaped to some degree.

When a prospect buys from you, they drop out of your funnel into the bucket below. This is where your active customers sit, who are the people or businesses you're currently helping, or that you help on a regular basis. They include customers who are still actively using what they bought from you the first time, as well as any customers who come back to buy from you repeatedly.

Your role as a salesperson might be to grow or develop the customers in your bucket further, or simply to protect and retain their existing level of business. Either way, there's a job to do because unfortunately all buckets are leaky.

Lapsed customers are people or businesses who've bought from you in the past, but who are no longer buying from you or actively engaging with the product or service they bought previously. They might have leaked out of your bucket because their needs have changed, or because something about you changed, which means your product or service is no longer a good fit. Or perhaps a competitor lured them away, so they now sit in their bucket and not yours. Whatever the reason, the important principle is that lapsed customers are not necessarily permanently lost. Your role as a salesperson might be to re-engage with and win back these lapsed customers by effectively dropping them into the top of your sales funnel again, which, contrary to popular opinion, is usually easier to do than it is to find, engage and convert a brand-new customer to replace them.

This funnel, sieve and bucket sales pipeline model is simple to understand and, as you'll see throughout this book, it can be a very powerful tool indeed.

Your role in the sales pipeline

Different sales teams have different roles at different stages of the sales pipeline, and not all sales teams are involved all the way through. Let's have a look at the different roles each of our three sales teams play.

The Drinkit sales team are involved at every stage of their sales pipeline.

- ▶ It's their job to actively find new potential customers by using a database of pubs, bars and shops provided by their employer; through conversations with their wholesale partners; and through their own active research. Once they've identified a promising lead, they then visit them in person to engage in conversation.

- ▶ After they've successfully opened a conversation, they continue to qualify whether they're a good fit for each other, and then present the right Drinkit products, in the right way, in order to try to close a sale.

▶ Once they've converted a prospect into an active customer, it's their job to continue to grow and develop that customer's account by helping them to sell more beer, and to retain and protect the customer from being poached away by a competitor.

▶ Finally, because every salesperson's bucket is leaky no matter how good they are, the Drinkit sales team are also tasked with approaching lapsed customers who've stopped buying Drinkit beer for any reason, to re-engage them in conversation and persuade them to buy Drinkit beer once again.

The SupportIT sales team's role is similar, but different.

▶ Like the Drinkit team, it's also their job to proactively find new potential customers. They do that through a combination of searching through a database of businesses, and through their own online research. They're also occasionally passed leads that have come in via the 'Contact us' page of their website. Once they've identified a lead, they reach out, typically by phone and email.

▶ When they've successfully opened a conversation and have qualified that they and the prospect are probably a good fit for each other, they're tasked to propose and present the right IT support solution, in the right way, to close a sale.

▶ However, unlike the Drinkit team, once the SupportIT sales team has closed a sale, it's not their job to develop and protect the active and repeat customers in their bucket. That job passes to the SupportIT customer care team, who are tasked with looking after customers once the initial contract has been signed.

▶ But, just as the Drinkit team are tasked with doing, the SupportIT sales team's role also includes actively approaching lapsed customers to attempt to re-engage them and win them back.

The Widget Store's sales team has just an important role, but they're not involved in as much of their organization's sales pipeline.

▶ At the Widget Store it's the marketing team who are responsible for reaching out to prospective customers via different advertising and marketing channels, including via TV, radio, social media and email.

▶ However, once a prospective customer comes into store, it's very much the sales team's role to build on that initial engagement, and to close sales through conversations that customers describe as being a great buying experience.

▶ The Widget Store's sales team have no way to continue the conversation with customers once they've left the store. However, they *are* tasked with getting customers to provide their email address and sign up for the Widget Store's free loyalty card, which then allows the marketing team to continue the conversation.

▶ As well as encouraging repeat custom, the loyalty card is key to providing the Widget Store's marketing team with a way they can potentially identify and reach out to lapsed customers, and attract them back into store.

Activity: Understand your sales pipeline

Review the sales pipeline from Figure 6 and reflect on your role.

▶ How much are you involved with the different types of customers and with the associated sales activities that sit alongside that section of the pipeline?

▶ If there's a section of the pipeline that's not your responsibility, whose responsibility is it? And do you fully understand how their role connects with yours?

▶ Are there any areas of your pipeline that could benefit from extra attention? If so, how could you make that happen?

▶ Is the top of your funnel wide enough? Are you actively identifying and engaging enough leads at the upper end of your pipeline? If not, how could you identify more, or increase your ability to engage leads effectively?

▶ What shape is your funnel? Does it narrow quickly because you're good at disqualifying and sieving out low-quality prospects for the right reasons? Or are you losing prospects from your funnel that you don't want to? If so, why, where are they going, and what could you do to stop that from happening?

▶ Do you have any prospects that get stuck in your funnel for long periods of time that you could, and should, convert more quickly?

▶ How do you grow and develop the active customers in your bucket?

▶ How leaky is your bucket, and what could you do to stem the flow of customers from it?

▶ Do you proactively look for and attempt to re-engage lapsed customers? If not, why not? If you do, do you do that quickly and effectively enough, or are there ways you could improve?

Make a note of anything you learn as you go through this process, because this can provide useful insight into how you could develop or improve your sales strategies and plans.

Chapter 10: Summary

Understanding your role in the sales pipeline is key to improving how you find, engage, convert and retain customers. This chapter has explored the different stages of the pipeline and highlighted how your actions at each point make a difference.

▶ A sales pipeline maps the journey from potential customer to lapsed customer, helping to align a customer's status with the required sales activity.

▶ The pipeline begins with suspects and leads, where the focus is on identifying, qualifying and opening conversations.

▶ Prospects sit within the funnel where conversations deepen, qualification continues and the aim is to close sales.

▶ Active customers fall into the bucket beneath your funnel, where your objective shifts to growing and developing, and protecting and retaining their business.

▶ All buckets leak, so re-engaging lapsed customers is an essential part of maintaining a healthy sales pipeline.

▶ Not all sales roles span the full pipeline. However, understanding each stage strengthens your ability to support others and improve your own effectiveness.

This model will help you to stay focused, structured and strategic as you move customers through your pipeline and grow lasting sales success.

Chapter 11
Your sales strategies and plans

Understanding sales strategies and plans

The terms *strategy* and *plan* are often used interchangeably. If you look at the dictionary definitions for each, it's easy to see why.

Strategy:

1. a plan, method or series of manoeuvres or stratagems for obtaining a specific goal or result: a strategy for getting ahead in the world; or

2. skilful use of a stratagem: the salesperson's strategy was to always seem to agree with the customer.

Plan:

1. scheme or method of acting, doing or making, etc., that's developed in advance, for example: a battle plan; or

2. a design or scheme of arrangement, for example: an elaborate plan for seating guests; or

3. a specific project or definite purpose, for example: plans for the future.

As you can see, the dictionary definitions don't really help to separate the two terms. For example, part of the dictionary definition for a *strategy* defines it as a *plan*! However, the two *are* different.

To highlight and explain the differences, I prefer to use the terms *strategic plan* and *tactical plan*.

The strategic sales plan

A strategic sales plan is usually developed by an organization's sales leadership team, rather than by the salespeople working at the sharp end of customer conversations. It describes, at a relatively high level, the approach the sales team will take in order to achieve their goal.

It's the sales equivalent of the marketing team's customer contact strategy, which defines who, how and what the marketing function will do to communicate with different types of customer at different stages of the sales pipeline. So it's important that the sales and marketing teams' strategic plans are closely aligned.

The strategic sales plan answers the question of 'Who…?', by referring to segments of the organization's target market rather than by describing specific individual customers. While the strategic sales plan touches on the question of 'How…?', it does so from a high-level perspective, defining the toolkit of approaches that may be used and the steps that may be taken. For example, the strategic plan will define the sales channels to be utilized (field sales, inside sales, retail stores, and so on), as well as the way that resources will be deployed within those channels. It may go further by describing the tools available and the steps to be followed, but it stops short of prescribing exactly when those tools and processes are to be deployed – that's the preserve of the tactical sales plan, which we'll come to shortly.

So there are three plans that all need to align: the marketing team's customer contact plan; the sales leadership team's strategic sales plan; and the salesperson's tactical sales plan. Like all good sales and marketing activities, each of these plans also needs to align with the customers' needs and wants too.

This might sound complicated, but one way to ensure this alignment is to structure each of these plans in line with the different stages of the sales pipeline, as this already groups customers differently depending on where they are in their buying journey.

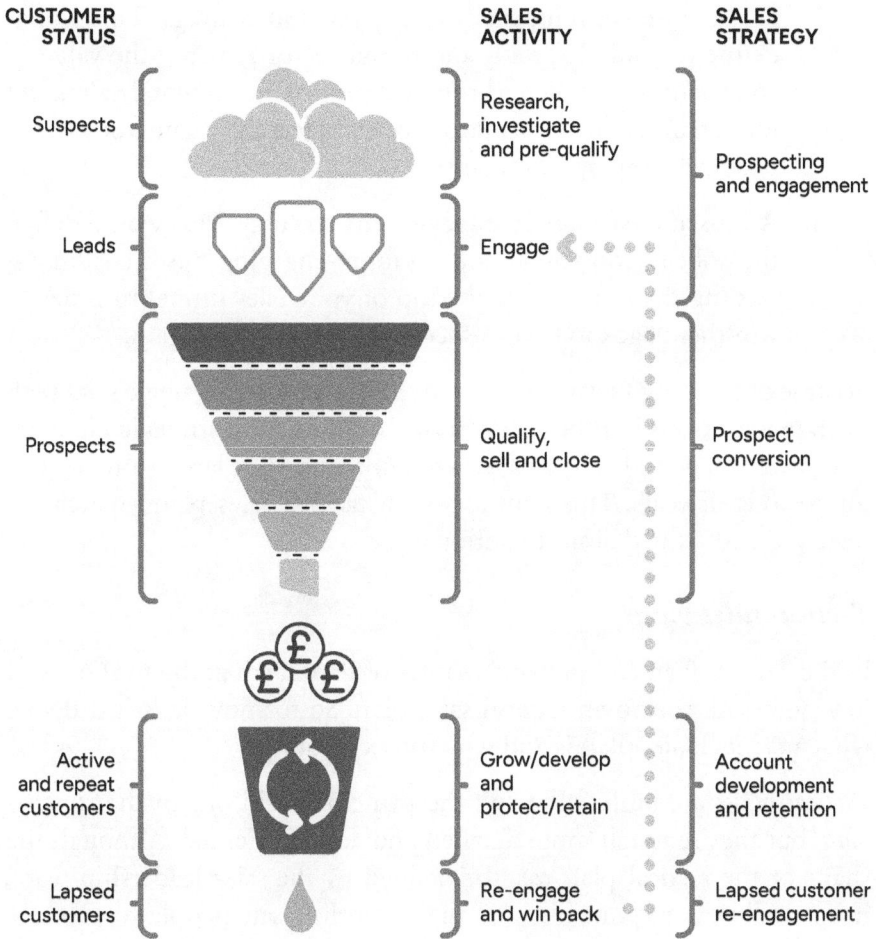

Figure 7: The pipeline-aligned sales strategy model

As you can see in Figure 7, which you can also view in higher resolution by going to greatersales.com/bookextras, a sales strategy that aligns with our sales pipeline model would have four elements, as follows.

1. **A prospecting and engagement strategy.** This would define the policies, tools and resources for actively investigating your pool of suspects, in order to identify leads and turn them into engaged prospects.

2. **A prospect conversion strategy.** This would define the policies, tools and resources for engaging and communicating with the prospects in your funnel, in order to move them down your pipeline and close sales to convert them into active customers.

3. **A customer development and retention strategy.** This would define the policies, tools and resources for growing the value of your active customers through repeat or incremental sales, and for retaining their business while protecting them from being poached away by your competitors.

4. **A lapsed customer re-engagement strategy.** This would define the policies, tools and resources for re-engaging lapsed customers, feeding them back into the top of your sales funnel in order to win them back to become active customers once again.

Because of their high-level nature, and the need for the strategic sales plan to align with plans in other parts of the business, most strategic plans are only reviewed periodically and tend to remain in place largely unchanged for periods of years. This contrasts with tactical sales plans, which are reviewed and refined almost continually.

Tactical sales plans

In the 'Step 1: Plan and prepare' chapter of Part 3, I'm going to show you how to create your own tactical sales plan. So for now, let's just define what a tactical sales plan is and why you need one.

Tactical plans are built following the principles laid out in the *strategic plan*, but they're much more detailed and action oriented. Although the shape of the tactical plan may be defined by the sales leadership team, it is usually the responsibility of their frontline salespeople to produce and refine it. One reason for this is that tactical sales plans include details for specific individual prospects and customers, and so each salesperson typically maintains their own plan for the group of customers or geographical territory they're responsible for.

A tactical sales plan is an action plan that tackles questions like who, how, when and what, by answering questions such as 'Who am I going to target when prospecting?', 'How am I going to use the different tools and resources made available to me?', 'When am I going to focus on targeting this particular type of customer?', and 'What are my underlying objectives for my customer conversations?' This means tactical plans are very dynamic and constantly changing, but they don't have to be captured within a single document. At the basic level, a salesperson's tactical plan might be driven by the objectives agreed during their last appraisal or review, and defined by the details held within their calendar, diary or CRM system.

Customer-specific sales plans sit at the sharp end of tactical plans. For salespeople dealing with short-chain sales and high volumes of customers, these customer-specific plans may not be documented – or where they are written down they might consist of just a few bullet points. In its simplest form, your customer-specific plan might simply consist of your list of target customers, with the objectives you want to achieve during your next conversation alongside each one.

In summary

Strategic sales plans	Tactical sales plans
Focus on long-term, high-level goals	Focus on short-term, detailed targets
Define the framework	Detail your action plan
Include policies, processes, tools and resources	Include prioritized tasks and diarized activities
Address groups of customers	Specify individual customers
Are owned by your sales leadership team	Are owned by you as an individual salesperson
Are reviewed periodically and changed infrequently	Are reviewed and refined continually

Defining your sales strategies and plans

Activity

Refer back to the sales pipeline in Figure 7. Take a moment to consider how the following four elements of a good strategic sales plan sit alongside it:

1. prospecting and engagement;

2. prospect conversion;

3. customer development and retention; and

4. lapsed customer re-engagement.

For each of these elements of your organization's strategic sales plan, make sure you know the answer to these questions.

> ▷ Whose role is it to enact this element of the plan within your organization?

▶ Why is that part of the strategic plan important to *your* goals, objectives, targets and KPIs?

▶ Where could you find information about the customers that element of the plan serves?

▶ When is the best time to contact those customers? What are the triggers?

▶ What policies, processes, tools and resources does your organization have available to help?

▶ How could you help to improve or better enact this element of your organization's strategic sales plan?

Knowing the answers to these questions will help you to build and improve your tactical sales action plan, and set customer-specific objectives. I'll show you how to do both of those things in detail in the 'Step 1: Plan and prepare' chapter of Part 3.

Chapter 11: Summary

To wrap up this chapter, here's a short summary of the key principles we covered that will help you to understand your organization's sales strategies, and develop more effective tactical plans.

▶ Strategic sales plans are high-level, long-lived frameworks created by the sales leadership team. They define how the organization will approach different groups of customers, and the policies, tools, resources and processes it will use to do so.

▶ Tactical sales plans are detailed, short-term action plans developed by individual salespeople. They focus on specific customers and day-to-day sales activities.

▶ Alignment is essential. Your tactical plan must be distilled from your organization's strategic plan, which must line-up with your organization's marketing plan. And, most importantly, all of these plans should align with your customers' needs.

▶ Your sales pipeline can help bring structure and clarity to all of these plans by mapping them to the different stages of your customer's journey.

▶ A good strategic plan typically includes four core elements: prospecting and engagement; prospect conversion; customer development and retention; and lapsed customer re-engagement.

▶ A good quality tactical sales plan also aligns with these four elements, defining the tasks, objectives, and actions for specific customers in each case. I'll show you how to create and optimize your own tactical sales plan in Part 3.

PART 3

WHAT YOU NEED
TO DO: THE SEVEN
ESSENTIAL STEPS
FOR GREATER SALES
CONVERSATIONS

Introducing the New 7-Step Sale

A sales process defines the sequence of steps that salespeople follow to guide them through a sale.

The origin of the formally defined sales process is somewhat lost in history. The earliest example of a personal selling process I've seen is from a 1920s training book entitled *How to Increase Your Sales*, by The System Company. They listed the six steps of selling as: (1) find the prospect; (2) pre-approach; (3) approach; (4) the demonstration; (5) the argument; and (6) the close.

The father of the seven-step process is widely credited as being Doctor Alan Dubinsky who, in 1981, published a study entitled 'A factor analytic study of the personal selling process'. In that article, Dubinsky listed seven steps of the sale, comprising: (1) prospecting; (2) pre-approach; (3) approach; (4) presentation; (5) overcoming objections; (6) close; and (7) follow-up. The only real difference from the process used in the 1920s being the addition of a seventh 'follow-up' step.

Fast-forward to today, and many sales trainers, books and courses, still refer to those original steps. But although these are solid foundations to build on, selling has changed a lot in the past 100-plus years, and so the sales process needs to evolve too.

The New 7-Step Sale

Throughout Part 3 I'm going to walk you through the steps of the New 7-Step Sale. These are: (1) prepare; (2) engage; (3) understand; (4) present; (5) trial close – and overcome objections or negotiate only if necessary; (6) close; and (7), follow-up.

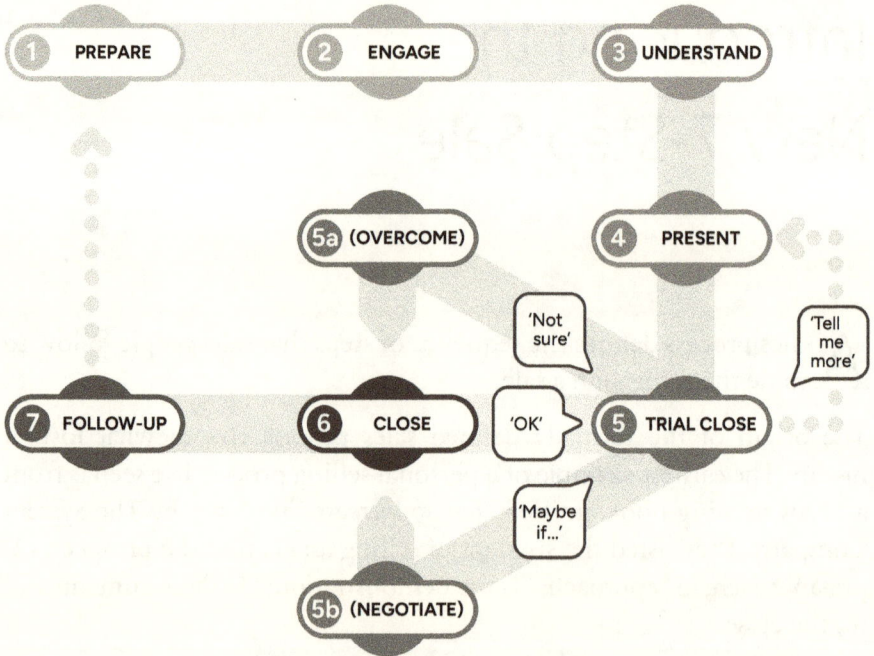

Figure 8: The New 7-Step Sale

As you can see from these steps and from Figure 8, although these seven steps are still built on the same solid foundations that have been in place for more than 100 years, the New 7-Step Sale is different in a number of ways.

▶ First, I've renamed some of the steps to better define what you have to do or achieve. For example, *pre-approach* becomes *prepare*, and *approach* becomes *engage*.

▶ Second, prospecting is no longer a separate step in the process, because it doesn't form part of every sales conversation or every salesperson's role. A good sales process should be as applicable for growing and developing existing customers as it is for engaging and winning new ones. So in the New 7-Step Sale, any initial prospecting actions now fall under the new first step of *prepare*, which covers everything you need to do prior to engaging a prospective *or* existing customer in conversation.

▶ I've added a new and important *understand* step between *engage* and *present* to capture the essence of modern consultative selling, and to convert the old 7-step process, which was based on how salespeople like to sell, into a process that's based on how customers like to buy. This new step also helps to combat the tendency some salespeople have to slip straight into delivering a practised and generic sales presentation. And it supports the principle that you can only sell what a customer values, needs and wants, if you take the time to understand them first.

▶ I've also added a new *trial close* step after the presentation. I'll explain this step in more detail shortly, but as you can see from Figure 8, this step allows you to pivot the sales conversation in different directions depending on how the customer responds. This is important, because a good sales process shouldn't be overly restrictive or lead to sales conversations that feel contrived. Customers, as well as salespeople, need to feel they have some agency in the process.

▶ I've moved the *overcome objections* step off the main process line to become Step 5a. I've done this to represent that, although it's a direction your trial close might take you, if you get the preceding steps right, it may not be something you need to do at all – and it isn't a step you should aim for.

▶ I've added a *negotiate* step into the sales process, as this is something many salespeople will need to do from time to time before they can close a sale. But just like handling and overcoming objections, negotiating isn't always required, nor is it something you should aim to do, so this too sits off the main process line as Step 5b. (It's Step 5b, because, as I'll show you, you should only open a negotiation if your initial attempt to overcome your customers' objections fails, which is Step 5a.)

▶ I've transformed the *follow-up* step from being just a tactical action that ends the sales process, into one that also drives continual improvement, by connecting it back to Step 1 to create a positive feedback loop. This is because an effective process involves reflecting on what you've learnt, and encourages you to apply that to create cycles of marginal gains that help you to get a little better every time.

▷ Finally, I've kept the main process to seven steps and have laid it out as a visual map to make it easy for you to remember and follow. This will allow you to focus on your customer as you both enjoy a conversation that *feels* natural – safe in the knowledge that at every point you know where you are, where you're heading and how to get there.

In the following chapters I'll define each of the steps in detail and show you exactly what you need to do to put the New 7-Step Sale into action. But before that, let's explore some of the benefits of this refined process.

The benefits of the New 7-Step Sale

Just as I have with the sales mindsets and knowledge in Parts 1 and 2 of this book, I've been teaching and refining the New 7-Step Sale for more than ten years, both directly with many hundreds of salespeople, and indirectly with thousands more via my online academy and my sales apprenticeship and diploma partners. So the process, and the tools and techniques that sit within it, are proven to work.

Here are some of the benefits I've seen as people have put the New 7-Step Sale into action.

Benefits for salespeople

When you follow the New 7-Step Sale, you'll find yourself:

▷ feeling more confident;

▷ having better, more natural sales conversations;

▷ speaking with prospects and customers who are much more engaged;

▷ having shorter, more focused sales conversations;

▷ experiencing prospects moving to close the sale themselves;

▷ never being tempted to resort to manipulative tricks;

- not worrying about closing;

- getting excited over higher win rates; and

- being thanked by customers for your help.

Benefits for sales teams

When all salespeople within a team follow the New 7-Step Sale, this brings additional benefits too.

- It promotes unity by providing a common language and framework that enables team members to share their learning and help each other more effectively.

- It makes it easier for managers and trainers to identify which part of the sales process they should focus on helping their people to improve, to maximize the return they get from their training investment.

- It helps everyone to better organize their learning and thinking, by providing a framework off which they can 'hang' all the different sales skills, tools and techniques they have available.

- And it helps to create an efficient, effective and consistent team that delivers greater sales results.

Benefits for customers

As you already know, greater sales conversations are ones where everybody wins. So when you follow the New 7-Step Sale, your customers will win too. Here are some of the benefits they'll receive.

- **Better value.** The New 7-Step Sale is underpinned by the value-add mindset. So the value you provide won't just be linked to the final product or service your customer buys; you'll be adding value at every step of the way.

- **A better understanding of their needs.** The New 7-Step Sale will help you to ask interesting questions, provide thoughtful insights and challenge customers to think differently – leading them to have a better grasp of their problems and opportunities, and of the possibilities they have to solve or capitalize on them.

▶ **Time savings.** Instead of lengthy research, your customers will benefit from your expert guidance to help them identify the right product, service and solution faster.

▶ **A personalized and enjoyable buying experience.** Although the New 7-Step Sale is a process, your conversations won't feel scripted or contrived. Instead, you'll lead customers through a conversation that feels naturally focused on them and their needs, where they'll play an active part in the journey, and will feel like a partner and co-creator of any final solution.

▶ **Increased confidence.** The New 7-Step Sale will help you to earn customer's trust, share deep knowledge and provide expert advice – leading your customers to feel confident about their buying decisions, and about the post-sales support they'll have access to.

Let's move on to look at each of the steps in detail, and I'll show how to put the New 7-Step Sale into action.

Step 1
Plan and prepare

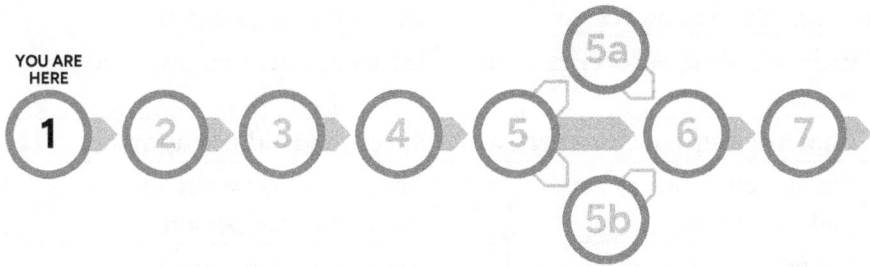

Figure 9: The New 7-Step Sale – Step 1

As Benjamin Franklin, one of the founding fathers of the United States famously said: 'By failing to prepare you're preparing to fail.' Or, as the British Army put it with their 7 P's maxim: 'Proper Planning and Preparation Prevents 'P' Poor Performance.' (I'll let you work out for yourself what the fifth 'P' stands for.)

Regardless of the source (and there are many), *planning and preparation* is widely deemed to be not just the first, but also the most important step to sales success.

While building the knowledge outlined in Parts 1 and 2 of this book could arguably be part of preparing for a successful sales conversation, that's the strategic end of the process. The *plan and prepare* step of the New 7-Step Sale covers the tactical side of putting that knowledge into action, from planning what you're going to do over the coming months and weeks, through to preparing effectively for a forthcoming sales conversation.

So in this chapter that's what you're going to learn: how to plan and prioritize your tactical sales activities, and how to prepare for an individual sales conversation.

Understanding tactical sales plans

You learnt about strategic sales plans in Part 2 of this book, so let's start by recapping the difference between a *strategic* sales plan and a *tactical* sales plan.

Strategic sales plans	Tactical sales plans
Focus on long-term, high-level goals	Focus on short-term, detailed targets
Define the framework	Detail your action plan
Include policies, processes, tools and resources	Include prioritized tasks and diarized activities
Address groups of customers	Specify individual customers
Are owned by your sales leadership team	Are owned by you as an individual salesperson
Are reviewed periodically and changed infrequently	Are reviewed and refined continually

Your *tactical* sales plan needs to follow the principles laid out in your *strategic* sales plan, but it needs to be much more detailed and action oriented. It needs to take the goals and principles from your strategic plan, and define the activities and actions you're going to undertake to achieve them.

Your tactical sales plan should define how you're going to split your time, energy and resources between engaging new prospects, converting prospects into customers, developing existing customer accounts, and re-engaging lapsed customers. But it should also go much further, by listing and prioritizing the individual prospects and customers you're going to focus on in each group.

Your tactical plan should identify the following.

A. Any actions you're going to take to research, investigate and qualify potential leads, to drive them into your sales pipeline.

B. The individual prospects you're going to target to convert into customers, and how you're going to prioritize your prospecting time and resources between them to maximize the return you're likely to get from that investment.

C. The individual customers you're going to target for growth and retention, and how you're going to prioritize your account management time and resources between them to maximize your ROI.

D. The lapsed customers you're going to target for re-engagement and win-back activities, and when and how you're going to contact them.

Hunters (who are salespeople primarily tasked with chasing new leads and converting them into new customers), will mainly focus on A and B, whereas farmers (who are salespeople primarily tasked with getting more business out of their existing clients) will primarily focus on C and D. But regardless of whether you're a hunter, a farmer, or both, at an organizational level none of those areas should be ignored completely.

Creating a prioritized sales plan

Prioritizing your prospecting activities

As you can see if you refer back to the sales pipeline in Figure 6, Chapter 10 – your prospecting and engagement actions sit right at the start of your sales pipeline. They involve researching and identifying potential future customers, pre-qualifying them by checking that they're actually a type of customer you could potentially help, then reaching out to these leads to turn them into engaged prospects. So prospecting refers to the act of creating engaged prospects, but doesn't involve the action of selling *to* those prospects in order to turn them into active customers.

Prospecting isn't something all salespeople have to do. If you take our three sales teams for example, only the SupportIT sales team are tasked with any prospecting activities. The Drinkit team are provided with pre-qualified leads in the form of a list of independent pubs and licensed retailers to visit, and the Widget sales team are faced with prospects who have pre-qualified themselves by deciding to visit the Widget Store. It's only the SupportIT team who are tasked with doing their own research and with making truly cold calls.

For this reason, I'm not going to focus on the skills needed for early-stage prospecting activities in this book, because it's not something every salesperson *needs* to do. But if researching, investigating and pre-qualifying leads *is* part of your role, then you need to include this in your tactical plan. Here's a simple but effective way to do that.

1. Plan when you're going to do your initial prospecting by blocking out time in your diary on a regular basis.

2. Specify where you're going to look, and how you're going to pick out and pre-qualify prospective customers from the pool of suspects you can access.

3. Set yourself a target for how many pre-qualified prospects you want to identify within a specific timeframe.

4. Review your progress against this target on a regular basis, and adjust your approach accordingly.

Prioritizing individual prospects and customers

While the only way you can prioritize your prospecting activities is to carve out time in your diary to complete them, when it comes to planning and prioritizing your prospects and customers you can take a much more detailed approach, because these are people or businesses you know more about.

You don't actually need much information to create a plan that shows which prospects and customers you're going to prioritize in order to maximize your return on investment. In fact, you only need to know three things. The first two things you need to quantify in each case are:

1. the existing value they currently provide for you; and

2. the potential value they could realistically deliver.

One way of quantifying this could be to evaluate the existing and potential level of sales you make to them. But a simpler way to do this is to give each prospect and customer a score from 0 to 10 against both metrics. For example, in terms of their existing value, you'd give a prospect you're not currently doing any business with a score of 0. And in terms of their potential value, you'd score them a 10 if they were the largest customer you could realistically land over the next few years.

As long as you're honest and consistent with your scoring across both metrics, this will allow you to quantify and compare every prospect and customer in terms of:

1. their current value; and

2. their growth potential (which you calculate by deducting their existing value from their potential value).

While this would be useful information to help you to create a prioritized plan of attack, it's missing one important factor. It doesn't address how *likely* it is that you'll retain their current level of business, or achieve any of that potential growth. This is why you need a third metric. You also need to know:

3. the strength of your relationship.

This needs to be a score that factors in both the strength of the relationship between you and the customer, and the strength of the relationship between your customer and the brand you represent. Both factors are important, because together they represent the likelihood that customer will buy, or will continue to buy, what you're selling.

In 'Step 7: Follow-up' later in this book, I'll show you how you can accurately measure the strength of your relationship, should you want to. But with practice, most salespeople can simply and effectively judge this for themselves, giving each prospect or customer a score between 0 (which could represent a prospect you haven't yet engaged), and 10 (which would represent an extremely loyal customer who wouldn't even think of buying from anyone else).

With these three scores – current value, potential value and strength of relationship – you now have enough information to rank your prospects and customers in order to create a prioritized tactical plan.

If you're focusing on growth, you can simply multiply each prospect or customer's growth score by their relationship score, then rank them all by the result to put your highest growth opportunities at the top.

Or if you want to focus on retention, you can look for customers with high current value scores and low relationship scores, to identify those who are at most risk of taking their business elsewhere.

The greater sales planning tool

I've developed a free tool you can use to create your own prioritized sales plan using the principles outlined here, which can combine both growth and retention objectives into one prioritized tactical plan.

By simply entering three scores against each prospect or customer (their current value, potential value and strength of relationship) this tool will help you to:

- ▶ see all of your prospects and customers ranked by their growth potential; and

- ▶ rank all your current customers from your most loyal through to those who are most at risk, in a way that takes their level of sales into account too.

However, this tool allows you to do much more.

- ▶ For each customer it combines their potential growth and potential risk into a single importance score, enabling you to create one plan that incorporates both your growth and retention objectives.

- ▶ It also enables you to fine tune your plan based on the strength of the market and your competitive position. When the market's buoyant and you're in a strong position, you can create a combined sales and retention plan that's more heavily weighted towards growth. Or, when there's uncertainty in your market or you're facing strong competition, you can create a plan that doesn't ignore growth, but upweights the importance of protecting your valuable customers.

- ▶ It also allows you to segment your prospects and customers into groups, perhaps based on their geographic location, or by the types of products or services they buy. This enables you to create smaller component plans that are each focused on a specific group of customers – helping you to prioritize which customers to call on when visiting a certain area for example.

You can download this powerful planning tool for free, and watch a video explaining how to use it, by visiting greatersales.com/bookextras.

Conducting customer research

In order to produce your prioritized tactical plan you will have had to complete some customer research. At the very least you'll have needed to pull some sales data and consider what you know about each customer in order to create their current value, potential value and strength of relationship scores.

Customer research is an important part of planning and preparation. Opening a conversation with a customer you know nothing about is a daunting task. You can also damage a relationship – or sabotage your chances of developing one – if you haven't bothered to find information that's easily available, and that the customer would reasonably expect an interested salesperson to know in advance.

Luckily, learning about markets and customers is now easier than ever, and you're likely to have a host of digital tools at your fingertips that are quick and easy to use. Here are some examples. As you run through the list reflect on which are available to you, which you could make better use of, and which might be worth investigating further.

Online and digital tools

These include the following.

- **Your inhouse CRM or sales engagement platform** – good for researching past interactions and customer histories.

- **The customer's website** – good for learning about their company updates, announcements and background.

- **Social media** – good for learning about the customer's interests, behaviour, current focus and engagement. Don't just focus on social media put out by their company; look at social media from their key people too. But remember, you're not a stalker! Focus on people's business-related accounts (such as their LinkedIn profile) or those they specifically intend to be publicly available. And avoid following or friend-requesting any account they might feel is more personal.

- **An online news search** – useful for finding recent news stories that feature the customer or their competitors. (Top tip: Set up a free Google Alert or AI scheduled research task for each of your significant prospects and customers. That way you'll never miss a news story that might provide an important engagement opportunity.)

▶ **AI and intelligent search engines** – especially useful for summarizing and helping to surface important information when there's lots available. Just be sure to check where the original information came from, so you don't rely on inaccurate, biased or even deliberately misleading sources. (Note that AI is a subject I'm going to come back to later in the book.)

Market research and intelligence tools

If you're selling to business customers, there are also tools that have been created specifically to help people like you. These include:

▶ industry reports;

▶ dedicated competitor analysis tools;

▶ industry news services; and

▶ financial and business information databases.

In summary

Customer research can be invaluable, but it can also be time consuming. So you must remember to apply your ROI mindset, and ensure that the amount of time and energy you're investing stays in proportion to the size of return you're likely to receive as a result. This is something the prioritized customer plan you created can help you with.

Also, remember that it's not just what you find out from your research that's important, it's what it means, and what you can do as a result to improve your chances of success.

Pay particular attention to any information that indicates a customer might be significantly different from those you're used to dealing with in some way, especially if this difference relates to their fundamental values or culture. To succeed in cross-cultural sales, salespeople need to be culturally aware, respectful and understand that different cultures have distinct communication styles. But you also need to avoid stereotypes. It's about understanding and respecting what their fundamental values probably mean, but also about reading and adapting to the customer in front of you. You'll learn more about how to do that as you progress through the New 7-Step Sale.

Setting conversation-specific objectives

Once you've produced your prioritized sales plan and have conducted additional research for the significantly important customers you're about to contact, you need to ensure you're well prepared for those forthcoming sales conversations.

This involves first assessing what you know about each customer by reviewing your plan and any research you carried out to build it, and looking back at any records from previous interactions they've had with you or your company. Then you can use that information to set yourself specific objectives for what you want to achieve out of that particular sales conversation.

Ideally, every sales conversation you have should directly contribute towards your sales objective – for example, by closing a sale and turning the prospect you're speaking with into an active customer. The problem is, that plan as you might, sales conversations often don't go exactly the way you want them to. When they don't (and they often won't), its important to know how you can still make the most out of the opportunity.

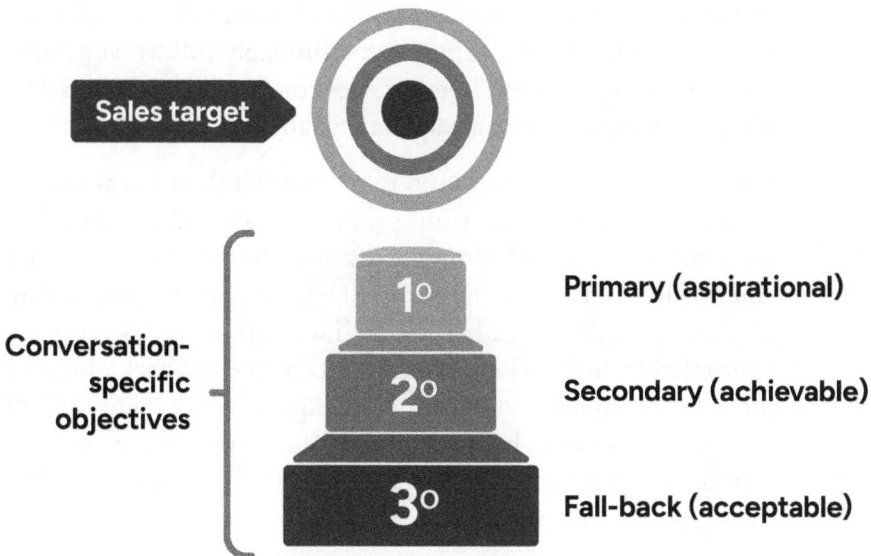

Figure 10: Setting conversation-specific objectives

For this reason, prior to any planned sales conversation it's important to take a few moments to set yourself three different objectives. These should be designed to give you a range of ways you could move forward, even if your prospect is more resistant, or perhaps even more embracing, of your proposal than you expected.

The three objectives you need to set yourself for each planned sales conversations are as follows.

1. **A primary objective.** This should be aspirational and stretching. This is the best outcome you could realistically hope to gain from your sales conversation. You should set primary objectives in the knowledge that you probably won't achieve them very often, but if you try, you will achieve them on occasion. As Norman Vincent Peale, author of *The Power of Positive Thinking*, said, 'Shoot for the Moon. Even if you miss, you'll land among the stars.'

2. **A secondary objective.** This is the more achievable 'star' you can still land on if your moon-shot falls short. This is probably the objective that your sales manager hopes you'll achieve. It's an objective that, in most cases, will directly contribute towards your sales target, and so will probably require some sort of sale, agreement or significant commitment from your customer. However, for the reasons I explained in Chapter 4, you probably still won't achieve your secondary objective in every sales conversation, which is why it's important for you to always have a fall-back.

3. **Fall-back objectives.** You need to set yourself these because even if you haven't achieved your primary or secondary objectives this time, there are still things you can do to increase the chance you'll achieve them in the future. However, setting yourself an objective simply to 'gather more information', or to 'improve your relationship', isn't enough. An acceptable fall-back objective should still require some form of change or active commitment from your customer, because in order to move the conversation forward, you need to move the customer closer towards a decision to buy, or buy-into, what you're selling.

An example of conversation-specific objectives

The Drinkit off-trade sales team's task is to maximize the volume of Drinkit beer sold through independent licensed retailers within their territory. So for a first visit to a prospective new customer, the objectives they set themselves might look something like this.

1. **Their primary and aspirational objective** could be for the retailer to permanently stock Drinkit Pale Ale in their fridge, selling both four-pack cans and individual bottles.

2. **Their secondary and more achievable objective** could be for the retailer to agree to sell Drinkit Pale Ale four-pack cans on a trial basis, starting with a small amount of free stock in a cardboard free standing display unit provided by the salesperson, but committing to buy more from their supplier if that stock successfully sells-through.

3. **One fall-back objective** could be to leave some free samples of Drinkit Pale Ale for the customer to try to discuss with their colleague, and agree a date when they'll return to discuss listing the product on either a trial or a permanent basis. (Note that gaining the customer's agreement to meet again on a specific date is key to achieving the objective, as this represents the customer moving mentally one step closer to making a buying decision.)

   Or, if the decision-maker wasn't available at the time of their visit, **another fall-back objective** could be to find out when they will be available, and get the member of staff on duty to agree to pass on their business card and sales brochure to the manager, next time they're in. Even though the salesperson didn't get to speak with the decision-maker, ensuring their details get passed on can still help to build the customer's awareness of them and their brand – which can be a good way to grease the wheels of a future sales conversation.

Setting other supporting objectives

You may also have other objectives for your sales conversations that would help *you* to move forward, but that don't require any form of active commitment from the customer. For example, you might want to obtain specific data or information that will help you to make a more targeted or personalized approach next time, such as knowing exactly who the final decision-maker is, what criteria they use to make sales decisions, or when their current competitor contract is due for renewal.

However, you need to see objectives like these as supporting objectives.

In the case of your primary and secondary objectives, achieving these should result in a sale, or in the customer buying into what you're selling. Whereas achieving any of your fall-back objectives should involve moving the customer one-step closer to what you hope will be a positive buying-decision next time. Setting supporting objectives in *addition* to these is OK, but they shouldn't replace your primary, secondary or fall-back objectives.

What happens if you don't achieve your objectives?

Setting yourself tiered primary, secondary and fall-back objectives will reduce the chances that you won't achieve any of the outcomes you were aiming for. But you can't eliminate the possibility of failure altogether, and neither should you try to. All of these objectives must be aspirational to some degree.

As I explained in Chapter 4, where we explored the decision-focused mindset, sales is as much about how you handle failure as it is about how you strive for success.

We built on this further when we explored the ROI mindset in Chapter 5, when I explained that, in terms of quantifying your return, you shouldn't discount the value of learning from failure. I'm going to show you how to do that when we explore the last step of the New 7-Step Sale, the follow-up, in a few chapters' time – because that step applies equally to the conversations where you *didn't* achieve your objectives, as it does to those where you *did*.

So although you *must* aim high, you must also accept that you're going to fail to achieve any of your primary, secondary or fall-back objectives on occasion too.

What's next?

Once you've completed your essential planning and preparation, it's time to move on to the second step of the New 7-Step Sale, to engage your customer and open a conversation.

Step 2
Engage your customer

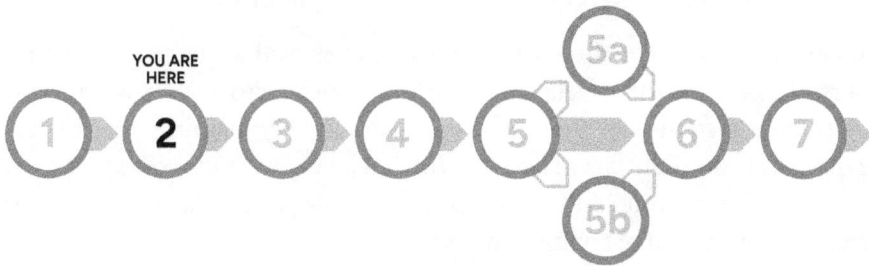

Figure 11: The New 7-Step Sale – Step 2

How to make a good first impression

Why is this important?

In 2006, Janine Willis and Alexander Todorov from Princeton University disproved the old adage that you only have seven seconds to make a good first impression. They did so by showing that for many key attributes, first impressions are not only made after just one-tenth of a second, but they're largely set in stone at that point too.

Their study, 'First impressions: Making up your mind after a 100-Ms exposure to a face', demonstrated that after just one-tenth of a second of seeing someone, we make snap judgements about their attractiveness, likeability, trustworthiness, competence and aggressiveness – all traits that are incredibly important to salespeople.

Not only that, but they also showed that the longer the initial engagement lasts, the more confident we tend to be that our original judgement was correct.

This effect is called 'thin slicing', which is the ability of our subconscious mind to find patterns in situations and behaviour based on very narrow slices of experience. If you think about how people really make decisions, which we covered in Chapter 4, you'll recognize that this is system-one at work – the processes in our brain that have evolved to make decisions quickly and automatically, without us even realizing it's happening.

If you consider the traits that the study found we make lasting judgements on extremely quickly (attractiveness, likeability, trustworthiness, competence and aggressiveness), you can see why it would have been an evolutionary advantage to make a quick call on these whenever we encountered someone new. Is this someone we should invite into our cave or keep out? Is the correct response to fight, flight or invite?

What's happening in these situations is that as well as judging the other person based on their facial features (and other factors such as hair and clothing), system-one processes are also quickly reading the micro-expressions on their face. These are tiny facial expressions you don't even know you're making, and they typically betray what you're thinking or feeling, even if you're trying to hide it.

For example, if you're feeling particularly confident or stressed it's going to show on your face, and regardless of whether your customer consciously recognizes it or not, they're probably going to pick up on it and make a snap judgement about what it means about you and your intentions. They'd probably just explain this as a gut feeling, but rather than being driven by their gut, they're being generated by their system-one processes at work in the background.

First impression top tips

If you want your customers to feel that you're likeable, trustworthy, competent and friendly (strong hint coming here – you do), then you need to put conscious effort into making a good first impression. But it's no good waiting until you're into your opening lines before you work on convincing them that you're the right person to help. You need to be doing that from the very first moment they see you.

Here are some tips to help you make those first few moments count.

1. Dress smartly – at least as smart, or even slightly smarter, than the smartest customer you expect to meet that day. But also dress appropriately. People like to buy from people like them – so if your customers are likely to wear a suit, you should dress professionally too. But if they're more likely to be wearing jeans and a T-shirt, smart-casual would probably be more appropriate.

2. Before you move into a position where your customer could potentially see you, take a few moments to get your head in the game before you make your approach.

3. Try not to take any strong emotions from previous sales conversations or recent events with you – particularly negative ones. Give them time to subside first. Listening to a playlist of music you find calming or uplifting can often help.

4. Believe. Believe in what you're selling – you know it's got features and advantages that you're confident will benefit your customer. Believe in why you're there – to help them make an informed buying decision by exploring and targeting win-win outcomes. And believe in your skills – I'm confident you've already got some selling skills even if you don't recognize them yet, and I'm going to help you develop those further as you move through this book.

5. Build your confidence by focusing on your objectives. You've already identified three different ways you can get value out of the conversation, even if things don't go as well as you hope they will this time.

6. Get your things organized, stand up straight and look forward. A straight posture signifies confidence and status, and catching someone's eye is a good way to show that you're interested.

7. Smile, but be genuine. Smiling makes people appear less threatening and more approachable, but system-one is incredibly good at spotting a fake smile, so focus on something that genuinely makes you feel pleased to be there. Incredibly, most people can even tell if the other person is smiling from the sound of their voice. So just like tips 2 to 6, this is something that can make a difference even if you're speaking by phone.

8. Be you. Customers want salespeople with character, and don't want robots who just regurgitate a practised script. So be polite, be professional, and follow the process – but make the sales conversation your own, and don't be afraid of injecting a bit of your own personality.

The confident engagement framework

If you're meeting your prospective customer face-to-face, your engagement started at the moment they first saw you. But if you're reaching out to your prospect by phone, this is where things start. Either way, your customer is expecting you to speak, so what do you say?

I'm going to give you a framework that will help you to open conversations confidently and effectively, but it's a framework and not a script. As you know, customers are incredibly good at spotting when a salesperson isn't being genuine, so I'll never put words in your mouth, and you shouldn't let anyone else do that either.

However, using a script that you create *for yourself*, based on the principles behind the confident engagement framework that follows, is absolutely fine. Here are the five principles you need to embrace.

1. **Get their attention.** A great way to do this is to say their name. Ever been in a noisy environment and caught someone you weren't paying attention to saying your name? Grabs your attention, doesn't it? So if you know their name, use it. If not, ask – then use it.

2. **Tell them who you are.** Customers like to know who they're speaking to, so give them your name and the name of the organization or brand you represent.

3. **Give them a personalized reason why you're calling.** Show them that they're important to you, ideally by saying something that you couldn't say to any other customer, at least not using those exact words.

4. **Hint at the benefit you can provide.** If this is a cold call (which it probably is if you're using this framework), then unless you can give them a reason why they should give you some of their time, they're probably just going to see you as an annoying interruption, and try to get rid of you as quickly as possible. Giving them a

clue about the benefit you could provide can help to keep them talking, and encourage them to engage further.

5.   **Ask them a question.** This step of the sale is about engaging your customer and opening a conversation, and the best way to do that is to ask them a question. One school of thought is that the first question you ask should be for a few minutes of their time. While this permission-based approach is respectful, the problem is that it's too easy for the customer to say 'No', and if you then continue, you risk being perceived as a pushy salesperson. So I recommend you come up with a quick *personalized* question that gets them thinking about the *value* you might be able to provide, and then ask it with confidence. You can then ask them for permission for a few minutes of their time as a follow-up question if necessary.

Let's look at how some of our salespeople might use this framework to open conversations with prospective customers.

Here's an example from the Drinkit on-trade sales team:

> *'Hi Olivia, I'm Drew from Drinkit. I wanted to come and see you because I've heard about the amazing Bike and Burger event you've got coming up to raise money for the Two Wheels for Life charity, and I thought that's an event we'd love to support. Do you mind if I ask, have you already got a drinks partner in place?'*

Drew's next step could be to ask for a few minutes of the customer's time, because if they *haven't* already got a drinks partner in place they're probably now wondering whether they should have, and so are more likely to agree. Alternatively, if they do have a drinks partner in place, it would seem natural for Drew to ask a follow-up question about who that is and whether there's scope for Drinkit to help too. At which point, Drew would have effectively opened the conversation by focusing on the customer and the value Drinkit could potentially provide.

Here's a different example from the SupportIT Sales team:

> *'Hi Daniel, I'm Alex from SupportIT. I'm calling because I saw your post about your new client win – congratulations on that by the way – and I wanted to see if we could help to protect the data you hold on them from hackers, as I know they often*

> *get targeted. I don't think you've got an IT team there, so can
> I ask if you've got anyone helping you with that yet?'*

Depending on their answer, Alex could *then* ask Daniel for a few minutes of his time to explore how SupportIT could help, as a next step.

Some might feel that not asking a permission-based question upfront is pushy, but I don't. Customers aren't afraid to let salespeople know when they're not open to a conversation, or simply don't have the time. If they do, pushing on with the conversation at that point *would* be pushy, but it shouldn't stop you from asking when would be a good time for you to call back, and whether you could book something in for then.

With practice, coming up with personalized opening lines like those doesn't take long, and they're so much more effective than just trotting out the same generic engagement script to every prospect you approach. But while these are scripts, the important thing is that they're *your* scripts, and because of that you'll find they trip of your tongue incredibly naturally.

The importance of ending on a question

Although I encourage you to try different ways to put the confident engagement framework into practice, it's important to always end with a question. As I explained when I introduced the New 7-Step Sale, one benefit of the 'understand' step (which is where you're going next), is that it helps to combat the tendency some salespeople have to slip straight into delivering a generic sales presentation.

That's probably the most common mistake salespeople make. They're so eager to tell the customer about all the different ways they can help, that they forget it's a sales *conversation*. So instead of talking *with* the customer, they end up talking *at* the customer, who quickly starts to become disengaged as a result.

What's next?

Another reason you need to end your engagement step with a question is because questions are key to understanding your customer, and that's the step we're moving onto next.

Step 3
Understand your customer

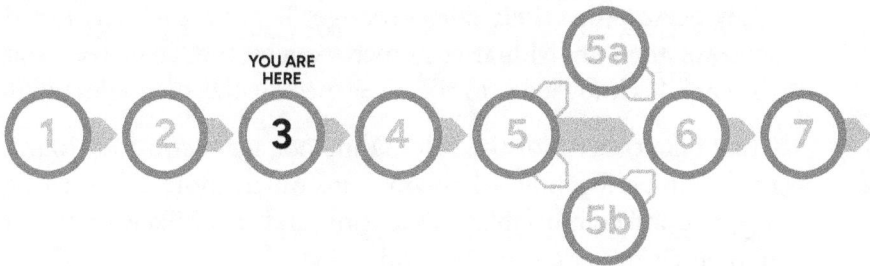

Figure 12: The New 7-Step Sale – Step 3

Take a challenging approach

The heart of the *understanding* step of the sales conversation is to ask questions and listen actively to what your customer has to say. However, before we look at how to do that, let's take a step back and consider the approach you should adopt as you do so.

In Chapter 1, I introduced the importance of balancing courage and consideration – balancing your courage to actively lead the sales conversation with consideration for the customer's needs. This concept is so important that it's embedded within our sales philosophy, to help people make informed buying decisions by *exploring and targeting* win-win outcomes.

This principle explains why, as a salesperson, not only is it OK for you to challenge customers (in the right way and for the right reasons), it should be something you wholeheartedly embrace.

This principle of challenging customers is explored in more detail in the 2011 book *The Challenger Sale* by Matthew Dixon and Brent Adamson. This book is based on a global study by the Sales Executive Council that examined the behaviours of more than 6,000 B2B salespeople. In the study, researchers found that the highest performing salespeople were much more likely to display the following behaviours.

- ▶ **They teach their customers.** They take the sales conversation beyond just the features of their solution, offering insights that provide a fresh perspective on the customer's situation. They also educate the customer – often revealing problems or opportunities the customer wasn't aware of.

- ▶ **They personalize their sales message.** They have a finely tuned sense of their individual customer's values and objectives, and they use this knowledge to effectively personalize their sales pitch.

- ▶ **They take control of the sale.** While not aggressive, they found that high-performing salespeople are much more likely to be assertive and comfortable with tension, and are unlikely to give in to their customer's every demand.

In short, the researchers found that although the best salespeople weren't pushy, they were often happy to challenge. Unsurprisingly, the researchers termed these salespeople *challengers*.

They also identified salespeople who were more *relationship*-led. Those salespeople focused on developing strong relationships with customers, were generous with their time, endeavoured to meet their customers' every need, and worked hard to resolve any tension. While those characteristics weren't necessarily absent in *challengers*, they weren't the skills and behaviours that defined a *challenger's* customer interactions.

In addition to *challengers* and *relationship builders*, the researchers also identified three other types of salespeople: *hard workers*, *lone wolves* and *reactive problem solvers*.

When they analysed the sales performance of these different groups, the researchers found that *challengers* accounted for almost 40% of the high-performing salespeople in the study and, as a result, *The Challenger Sale* book focuses on how salespeople can develop these characteristics. But as good as that advice is, it's not the full story.

Considering complexity

The study also noted that when the researchers cut the data by complexity of sale, separating out product-selling reps from complex solution-selling reps, they found that *challengers* increasingly dominated as the sales process got more complicated.

This is an important insight that often gets overlooked.

Frontline salespeople like you, typically sell through a single or short chain of sales conversations, with a single or short chain of decision makers. The sales you make are no less difficult and no less important than those of your long-chain peers, even if the sales conversations you have and the solutions you propose *are* less complex.

So although the study shows it's always more effective to challenge than it is to just blindly comply with your customers every request, the degree to which you challenge is important. The more complex your sales conversations and solutions are, the more important it becomes to challenge your customer's pre-existing ways of thinking.

What you need to do

You need to ask questions that challenge your customers to think differently, and it's OK to pepper your questions with facts and insights about the market or about your customer's competitors – if that helps. You also need to be prepared to respectfully challenge customers if they don't agree with your proposal, and I'll explain how to do that when we look at handling and overcoming objections in Step 5a.

But you need to recognize that challenging is not the same as pushing. Don't try to push customers into your way of thinking; it's good to influence and persuade, but it's never OK to bully or manipulate.

Balance your courage to lead the sales conversation with consideration for the customers needs. Don't be pushy, but don't be a push-over either.

The benefits of asking good questions

Challenging your customers to think differently is just one benefit of asking good questions in a sales conversation, but there are many more. For example, asking good questions could help you to do the following.

- ▶ **Build credibility.** Asking the right questions in the right way can help you to build your credibility and begin to establish yourself as an expert and trusted advisor, which is ultimately how you want your customers to see you

- ▶ **Fully qualify your prospect.** Good questions can help you to ensure no barriers exist that would prevent your prospect from buying from you, even if they wanted to.

- ▶ **Identify commonality.** Once people realize they have similar interests, desires or goals, they feel like teammates – and we're much more likely to agree with people we feel are 'on our side'.

- ▶ **Learn your customer's language.** People often use different words and phrases to describe the same thing. When people don't use the same language we do, we feel like they're an outsider, and not 'one of us'. Think about all the different words people use instead of 'employees' or 'profit' for example. Asking good questions can help you to learn the terms your customers prefer.

- ▶ **Learn about relevant buying experiences.** For example, have they had any past experience of your products or services? Or do they have an active relationship or any experience of your competitors? If so, what did they like or dislike about those experiences?

- ▶ **Avoid assumptions.** You probably know that to assume risks making an 'ass' out of 'u' and 'me', and that an assumption is often the mother of a screw-up. Asking good questions can help you avoid these mistakes.

- ▶ **Highlight known pain.** In sales terms, *pain* refers to the problems a customer has. Your prospect might already know that they have problems you could help them solve, but asking the right questions can still help to highlight the seriousness of these, and can potentially inject a bit of urgency into their desire to move forward.

▶ **Uncover hidden pain.** Good sales questions can also help to uncover problems that your customer didn't know they had, and help them to recognize potential future problems you can help them avoid too.

▶ **Dig for root causes.** To make a sale you need to understand the problems you can help your customer to solve or avoid. But sometimes the cause of the problem isn't clear, or perhaps it isn't what they assume it to be. Sometimes challenging people about what's causing their problems isn't a comfortable experience, and for the customer, the digging – and the ultimate discovery itself – might not be pleasant either. But customers typically care far more about the value they get from the sales process and what they're buying, than they do about the person selling it to them. Your role as a salesperson is to be an expert and trusted advisor, not a friend. So don't be afraid to dig if that's going to help you to add value.

▶ **Make it more likely your prospect will agree to your future proposal.** In his 2016 book entitled *Pre-Suasion: A Revolutionary Way to Influence and Persuade*, Doctor Robert Cialdini describes pre-suasion as the process of arranging for a recipient to be sympathetic to a message *before* they experience it. This might sound like some sort of magic, but asking good sales questions can help you to do just that.

▶ **Allow you to move naturally into your sales presentation.** Done right, all of the customer-facing steps of the New 7-Step Sale – from engagement right through to closing – should feel like a natural and seamless conversation. Experiencing a salesperson clunkily 'change gear', as they move from 'talking with' to 'selling at' a prospect, can be a jarring and unnerving experience. And in some cases, it can immediately destroy the connection and rapport they've worked hard to build. Asking the right questions, in the right way and at the right time can help you to avoid that, and help you to move seamlessly on to the next step of your sales conversation.

So there are many reasons why you need to master the art of asking good questions. Let's move on to look at how to do that.

Basic question types

Before we look at how to ask questions that can get you where you want to go, let's explore the different types of questions you can ask, and why they might be useful.

Open and closed questions

In basic terms, a question can be either open-ended or closed-ended.

Open-ended (or 'open') questions are good for getting prospects and customers to talk and share general information. As you might expect from the name, the type and length of answer you can expect to receive from these questions is somewhat open to interpretation, because open questions don't solicit a specific type of answer.

Open questions tend to start with: 'Who…?', 'What…?', 'Why…?', 'Where…?', 'When…?', 'Which…?' and 'How…?'

Closed-ended (or 'closed') questions are the opposite, in that they're good for closing down the types of possible response you might receive, and can help you to get short, specific answers.

Closed questions typically start with verbs such as 'Are…?', 'Is…?' or 'Did…?' For example, 'Is this a good time to talk?' or 'Did you get the email I sent you last week?'

Any question that would be naturally answered with a 'yes' or a 'no' is a closed question. However, another example of a closed question would be one that begins 'How many…?', because the way this question is phrased also closes down the types of answers you'll probably receive in response.

Why it's important to phrase questions carefully

An example of an open question would be: 'What do you think will be your biggest challenge this year?'

Unless a customer is being particularly awkward, you're likely to get a reasonable amount of information in response – especially if you pause to encourage them to expand if they give you a really short answer. So this could be a good question to use early in the *understanding* step of your sales conversation, as it could initiate a discussion that would help you to learn more about your prospect.

Compare this with a seemingly similar question: 'Is there a specific challenge that's holding you back?'

That's technically a closed question, as it effectively closes down the answers you might get to a 'yes' or a 'no'. Of course, if they said 'Yes', it would be relatively easy to get them to expand on that further by asking the obvious follow-up question. But there's always a risk they could say 'No', which might make things awkward, and could risk derailing your conversation altogether.

This helps to explain why it's usually a good idea to focus on asking open questions during the early stages of the *understanding* step. But there are exceptions. Since open questions can lead to long-winded answers, they can be poor tools for getting specific information, and sometimes, in the early stages of your conversation, that's exactly what you need.

For instance, if you want to qualify whether a business is large enough for you to work with, you probably wouldn't find out by asking what its biggest challenges are. But you might if you ask, 'How many people work here?'

Probing questions

While open questions are good for drawing out information, there are certain questions you can use to help you probe more effectively when you want to gain a deeper understanding. A good example of these are TED questions such as:

- ▶ **T**ell me…

- ▶ **E**xplain to me…

- ▶ **D**escribe for me…

Asking TED questions needs confidence, because when they're properly phrased, they aren't really questions at all, they're instructions.

But the mistake many salespeople make is to shy away from using them as they should, by turning them back into a question, essentially negating much of their impact. For example, anything that starts with 'Can you tell me…?', is technically a closed-ended question, and although you're unlikely to get just a 'yes' or 'no' in response, you'll likely receive a more detailed answer if you use the more direct 'Tell me…' alternative.

When delivered in the right tone, with confidence, and as a way of probing more deeply into information that a prospect has already started to share, TED questions can be very effective. Here's a simple activity that can help to prove the point. Ask someone about a journey they took using the following open question: 'How did you get here?' Then follow-up using the TED question: 'Describe the journey for me', and notice the difference in the two answers you receive.

How to ask questions to get where you want to go

Curiosity is a great way to build rapport in almost any situation, and good salespeople are curious even about matters that don't directly relate to the products or services they sell.

One of the best ways to display genuine curiosity and interest during any conversation is to listen carefully, pick up on points the other party has raised, and ask insightful follow-up questions. Prospects – like most people – appreciate it when a salesperson shows a genuine interest in things that are important to them, *especially* when they're not directly important to the salesperson.

However, as useful as a naturally flowing rapport-building conversation is, your questioning needs to have both *purpose* and *direction*.

As we've already explored, there are lots of reasons why you should ask your prospects and customers questions, but the primary purpose is to help you understand their needs and wants that you could potentially satisfy, and any problems you could help them to solve or avoid.

So as well as feeling like part of a naturally flowing conversation, your questioning needs to actively guide you towards the next step of your sales conversation, when you'll *propose and present* a solution to the problems you've discovered.

Using a questioning funnel

The best way to give your understanding step a structure that feels natural, meets all the objectives we've explored and allows you to move almost seamlessly into the presenting step, is to use a questioning funnel.

Question type	Example	Purpose
OPEN	Who? What? Why? Where? When? Which? How?	Open a conversation and draw out information
PROBING (Tell, explain, describe)	'Tell me more about...'	Gain deeper and specific understanding
CLOSED AND LEADING	'It sounds like you're looking for...' 'You want to avoid...'	Check and confirm (and highlight pain)

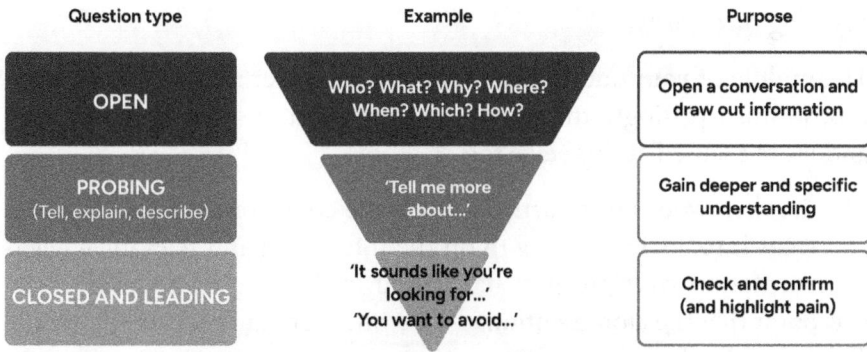

Figure 13: The questioning funnel

Open questions

As Figure 13 shows, the top of your questioning funnel is when you should predominately focus on asking open questions, because open questions are good for opening conversations and drawing out information.

While the nature of those questions will be fairly broad (hence why they're at the broad end of your funnel), they can still have context; demonstrate a certain level of preparation, insight or understanding; and (as far as possible if this is the first conversation you've had) can still be personalized to the specific prospect or customer you're speaking with.

The next question you ask might depend on your prospect's answer, which means listening closely and intently to how they reply. You might continue to build rapport by asking a follow-up question about something they said that piqued your curiosity, but isn't directly related to why you're there. Or you might ask an open-ended question on a different subject that's still broadly related to your potential common ground, as you continue to explore the different possible directions that your sales conversation could go.

But you need to ask mutually relevant questions which mean that at some stage soon, you'll likely hear something within their replies that's not only interesting, but can also be related to the product and services you sell and, more importantly, can be linked to a solution that you could propose and present to them shortly. When that happens, it's time to move the conversation forward by dropping down to the next level of your questioning funnel.

Probing questions

The middle of your questioning funnel is narrower than its broad, open top, so unsurprisingly the nature of your questions becomes narrower and more focused at this stage too.

This is where you start to actively guide the conversation towards where you want it to go, by homing in on the interesting and relevant nuggets of information your prospect has shared in their earlier answers. It's at this point that the aforementioned TED questions are particularly useful: 'Tell me..'; 'Explain to me..'; 'Describe for me..'

By asking specific questions like these, you can start to focus your prospect's thoughts on the aspects of their situation that are most important to both of you. This helps to identify commonality and highlight the complimentary nature of your situations, and starts to suggest there might be an outcome where you can help each other.

Carefully crafted probing questions can also give you opportunities to sow the seeds for ideas that could blossom into hidden 'wants' as you deliver your sales presentation – features and benefits your solution can provide that they didn't know they wanted until they heard they were possible.

Probing more deeply into specific areas can also help to highlight your prospects known pain, and uncover hidden pain points they didn't previously know they have. These pain points can be key when you move to the final stage of your questioning funnel.

Closed questions

Your objectives for this final narrow stage of your questioning funnel are to:

1. demonstrate that you've been listening and that you're focused on their situation, not just your agenda;

2. clarify and confirm that you fully understand their needs;

3. re-highlight the pain points you've uncovered (that you're about to help them solve); and

4. naturally close off your questioning and lead the prospect seamlessly into your sales presentation.

This is where closed and leading questions become particularly important. You can accomplish all of these objectives by asking leading questions that begin with statements such as:

- ▶ 'So am I right in thinking that...?'
- ▶ 'It sounds like you're looking for...?'
- ▶ 'I imagine you'd like to avoid...?'

Once you've used questions (or rhetorical questions) like these to check and confirm you understand their situation, it's the most natural thing in the world for you to segue into the next step of proposing and presenting your solutions to their problem. In fact, if you get these questions right, that's exactly what they'll want you to do next.

Why the questioning funnel works

One of the reasons this technique works so well is because it aligns with *Social Penetration Theory*. First proposed by Irwin Actman and Dalmas A. Taylor in their book *Social Penetration: Development of Interpersonal Relationships*, Social Penetration Theory explains that humans like to reveal information in layers. They equate it to peeling an onion: only when the outer layer is peeled back is another deeper level of information revealed.

So not only does the questioning funnel work because it helps you to structure your questions into different levels of detail, but also because that's the way humans feel most comfortable when disclosing information – especially information that might make us feel vulnerable.

Building a mental question bank

While you shouldn't enter into a sales conversation with a pre-determined list of questions you're going to ask come what may, it can still be useful to create your own mental question bank that you can refer to for inspiration.

One reason for this is that having some killer questions ready to pull out if the conversation stalls can help you to actively listen as your prospect answers your previous question, instead of switching off while you try to work out what you're going to say next.

Nobody should write these questions for you, because they need to be questions you're comfortable asking, phrased in a way that feels natural to you and your customers. However, as it isn't easy to come up with good quality sales questions, I've created some resources to help and inspire you. Like all of the images and resources listed in this book, you can access these for free by going to greatersales.com/bookextras.

What's next?

Closing your understanding step with a closed-ended question helps to ensure your customer is not only ready, but now actively *wants* you to recommend a solution to the problems you've just explored. So let's move on to look at how to do that.

Step 4
Propose and present

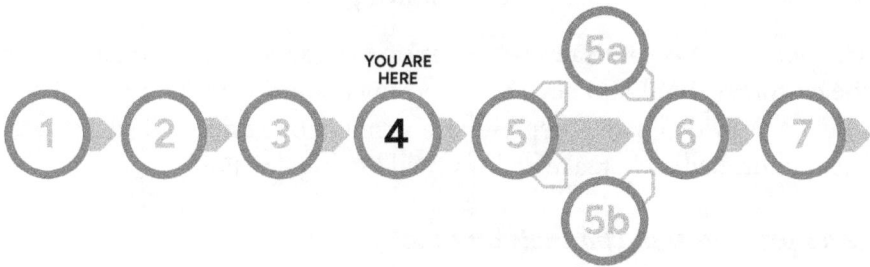

YOU ARE
HERE

1 2 3 **4** 5 5a 5b 6 7

Figure 14: The New 7-Step Sale – Step 4

Sales presentation objectives, channels and tools

Your objectives

Depending on the needs of the customer and the context of the conversation, sales presentations can be delivered in many ways, from simple verbal delivery to elaborate and interactive demonstrations. However, all sales presentations can be summed up in two words, because every sales presentation should be a *personalized recommendation*.

So you're not just going to present information. You're going to:

1. actively propose what the customer should do next;

2. justify your proposal by delivering a short presentation that's personalized to the customer's individual needs; and

3. stay in line with your underlying sales philosophy – helping the customer to make an informed buying decision by targeting a win-win outcome.

However, there's one more factor you need to consider when setting an objective for your sales presentation.

In the world of short-chain sales, once a salesperson has actively engaged a prospect, has taken time to understand their needs, and has proposed and presented a solution, if that specific conversation comes to an end without the prospect making a buying decision, the probability of closing the sale at a later date drops significantly.

So your objective should also capture this desire to encourage the customer to come to a decision *immediately* following your presentation.

The objective for your sales presentation is to actively recommend what the customer should do next, by proposing a solution that's personalized to their individual needs, represents a win-win outcome, and encourages them to immediately make an informed buying decision.

Sales presentation channels and tools

The channels through which a salesperson can appropriately and effectively deliver their sales presentations vary from one industry to another. But your objective to help the customer come to an *immediate* decision means the most appropriate and effective channels are those that can facilitate a live and interactive conversation.

It's common for short-chain salespeople to propose and present solutions in-person, by phone or in virtual meetings, and it's not usually appropriate or effective to do so solely via written documents or emails. Yes, text and visuals may be used to aid the sales process, but the sales conversation usually takes place live and in the moment.

So in this chapter I'm going to focus on techniques that will help you to deliver sales presentations primarily using your voice, but I'll also show you how you can use documents, visuals, props or other tools to aid and support your presentation where appropriate.

Approaching things this way also means that as long as you haven't lost your voice, you'll always have everything you need to propose and present a solution. Of course, if you find sales aids useful, you should always be prepared and have them available. But if ever you forget something, find yourself having to deliver a presentation unexpectedly, or have a piece of technology fail you (which often only happens at crucial moments), then you'll still be ready and able to present effectively.

How to deliver a FAB sales presentation

FAB sales presentations are fabulously engaging and compelling because they utilize the Features, Advantages and Benefits cycle we explored in Chapter 3. Here are the steps you need to take to deliver one.

1. Decide what you're going to recommend the customer does to resolve or prevent the pain points you uncovered and highlighted during the previous *understanding* step of your conversation.

2. Select the key features of your solution that you believe this particular customer is going to find most advantageous and beneficial – at least three, but no more than five – and put these in order.

3. *Propose* what the customer should do to resolve their pain and prevent future problems by ensuring they don't miss out on the benefits your product or service will provide. Then *present* a fabulously clear, succinct and compelling case to justify your recommendation.

4. Move on to the next step of your 7-step sales conversation, the *trial close*.

Let's look in more detail at putting those steps into practice.

Step 1: Decide what you're going to recommend

This step of the sales conversation is called the *propose and present* step, so you've got to be clear about exactly what you're going to *propose* the customer buys or buys-into, because that's where your sales *presentation* is going to start.

Some salespeople are able to tailor-make bespoke solutions for their customers by carefully selecting a blend of products or services from the range at their disposal. Other salespeople are tasked with selling a single product or service with little or no scope to make changes to it.

Whichever camp you fall into, this first step is for you to be clear on *exactly* what you're going to recommend your customer does. Your job is not to present the customer with options. If you want to explore a range of different ways you could potentially help the customer, that's what the *understanding* step is for. Use the *understanding* step to diagnose the problem, and the *presenting* step to prescribe your recommended solution.

To underline just how important this is, imagine you visit a medical consultant who diagnoses you with a serious and painful condition. How might you feel if they present you with a range of options and leave it up to you to decide what to do? Even if there were potentially different treatments available, you'd at least want to know their expert opinion and get their recommendation. So you need to do exactly the same for your customers.

Step 2: Select the key features you're going to highlight

It doesn't matter whether your solution can be tailor-made from a range of options, or whether the product or service you sell is more from the 'off-the-peg' end of the spectrum because, as you learnt in Chapter 7, you're always selling a package that consists of multiple features, advantages and potential benefits. So you can always deliver a bespoke and personalized sales presentation by focusing on the features and advantages that best align with this customer's values, needs and wants.

If you completed the suggested activities in Chapter 7, you'll already have a big list of features and related advantages that you *could* present – probably far more than you could reasonably cover in any sales presentation.

So your first task is to select which features and advantages are relevant for this customer, and which are not. If you're still left with a long list of relevant features (and you probably are), the next step is to decide which ones are likely to be most important and emotive for this specific customer. Which are the features and advantages that are most likely to motivate and influence them to buy into your recommended solution?

With practice, this is something that you'll do automatically during the understanding step. As you ask questions and listen actively to the answers you receive, you'll mentally highlight those features that are most important, and strike-through those that are irrelevant or could even damage your chances of successfully closing the sale.

Human brains tend to be drawn to even numbers because they feel balanced, symmetrical and complete. You see this preference in every-day life when people tend to organize things in pairs, or into groups of even numbers. But the opposite is true when it comes to decision-making.

When we're making decisions, most people find considering an odd number of points tends to be easier, because it helps to avoid indecision and makes our conclusions more clear-cut. With an odd number to choose from, especially three, there's a natural sense of progression and hierarchy, with one point often standing out as the deciding factor. Three is also the sweet spot for memory and attention – it's enough to convey meaningful information without overwhelming the listener.

So I recommend you optimize your presentations by focusing on three key features, because that will help you to keep your message simple, and make it easy for your customer to remember and act on. Presenting five key features can be OK if they're not overly complicated, but don't focus on any more than that.

Once you've decided on the key features you're going to present to justify your recommended solution, put them in order and start with the most important one – the one that gives context to the rest of the features you'll present – or the most beneficial one. Starting here will mean the *primacy effect* will work in your favour. The primacy effect is a mental bias that explains why people tend to remember and give more weight to information that comes first, than they do information that comes later. It also helps to explain why the first impression you make during the engagement step is *so* important and persistent.

A note on price
It's important to recognize that your customers don't care about the *price* of your product or service. What they care about is whether the *value* they'll get from it is worth the price you're asking, and whether their *budget* is sufficient to cover the price they'll have to pay.

Value and *budget* are things you should have explored with the customer during the *understanding* step of your conversation. You could do this perhaps by asking questions about: (1) what they're currently paying for similar products or services; (2) how much they feel the problem they want to solve is costing them; or (3) what their expectations are in terms of the profit or return they expect to receive if they were to invest in a new solution.

Once you understand what a customer's value and budget needs are, if the price of your product or service is important and isn't something the customer already knows, you can position it as a feature that helps to meet those needs as part of your presentation.

I'll show you some examples of how you can do that later in this chapter.

Step 3: Propose and present your solution

'I recommend...'

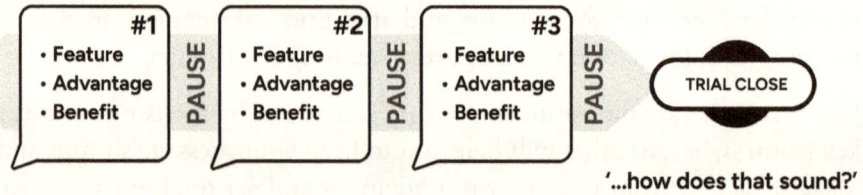

Figure 15: The FAB sales presentation framework

Figure 15 shows how you're going to pull all of this together to propose your recommended solution, and deliver a FABulously clear, succinct and compelling sales presentation to back it up.

In a moment I'm going to give you some examples of how our different salespeople put this model into action. But before I do that, let's look at how to build your presentation by breaking it down into its component parts.

You need to start your presentation by proposing *exactly* what it is that you believe your customer should do. You need to do this as clearly and succinctly as possible, and ideally in just one sentence.

You can see this in Figure 15 as the 'I recommend...' statement at the very top, because that's the language I like to use. You can use a word that's different from 'recommend' if you like, but you need to be confident and assertive. Not pushy. You're not going to 'demand' that your customer does something, but you do need to use words that demonstrate you have the courage of your convictions.

Clearly articulating your recommended action up front is important, because you don't want this message to get lost. The remainder of your sales presentation is simply to expand on, and justify, why you think this is the best outcome or way forward for you both.

Next, you need to justify your recommendation by presenting the different features you've selected to focus on, one by one, using clear *feature-advantage-benefit*, or 'FAB', cycles. Each cycle is simply a one- or two-sentence statement that introduces the feature, outlines its advantage, then explains why it will specifically benefit the customer.

You're going to present three of these cycles, one for each feature you've selected, and you're going to start with the feature that's most fundamental to your proposal, or most beneficial for this specific customer.

For each cycle, you're going to explain the key feature, then link it directly to its advantage and benefit using simple linking words, like this.

- After your initial 'I recommend..' statement, use the word 'because..', to segue into a one sentence explanation of the first feature of your recommended solution.

- Then use a phrase that starts with words like 'This means that..', and briefly describe the generic advantage of that feature.

- Finish this first FAB cycle by saying something like 'And that would help you to..', then link back to one of the problems the customer wants to solve or avoid, ideally by explaining the benefit using words you heard the customer say during the understanding step of your conversation.

You then need to pause, just for a second, before you give them another reason to buy into your proposal by presenting your next FAB cycle, saying something like this.

- 'This also..', then briefly explain the next feature your recommended solution has, is, does or comes with.

- Then say 'So it..', and give the generic advantage of that feature.

- Now finish this second FAB cycle by saying something like 'which would..', then briefly outline why that feature would benefit the customer too.

At this point, you need to pause again, just for a second, before laying another reason to buy on top of that. You do this by delivering your third, and probably final, FAB cycle of your presentation.

For simple sales presentations, that's all you need to do. So you could then move on to the next step of the New 7-Step Sale by asking a trial close question such as: 'How does that sound?' – which is something we'll look at in more detail in the next chapter.

This breakdown of the FAB sales presentation framework might sound complicated, and it does take practice, but when you put it all together in the right way, you end up with something that's simple for the customer to follow, but is incredibly powerful and persuasive.

FAB presentation examples

Here are some examples of FAB presentations from our different salespeople to show you just how effective this framework can be. In each case I've split their short speech into sections to help you identify the initial proposal, the three FAB cycles of their presentation, and the trial close question they end with. See what you'd think if you were the customer on the receiving end of one of these:

A Drinkit FAB sales presentation

'I recommend that rather than going with our pale ale on draught, we start by getting our 330ml bottles into your fridge.

'The reason I recommend starting there is because our bottles are widely available, which means you can get them through your existing wholesaler, and I know that would help you while you're tied-in with them until you change supplier in the summer.

'By listing our 330ml bottles now I can also get you some free POS, so I could get some glassware sent over, which would help you with your current shortage.

And this would also get you onto the benefits programme now, so by the time the summer comes you'd have some points built-up ready for when the big-ticket items are released – great for you because that could help you to get the parasols you're after for your beer garden.

'How does that sound?'

A SupportIT FAB sales presentation

'I recommend we enrol you onto our Bronze- level support plan,

because that's just £10 per user per month, which means it doesn't cost any more than your current solution, and so would come in within your budget.

'*The bronze plan also includes protection for all of your devices, so the tablets and phones your team have that are currently at risk would also all be protected moving forward.*

'*And as the account holder, you'd also have access to our 24/7 IT support service, which would be great for when you're working late or at weekends.*

'*How does that sound?*'

A Widget FAB sales presentation

'*I recommend you go for the Sumsang Q800 TV,*

because it has their new super-bright SDR screen, which means it looks great and prevents on- screen reflections in even the brightest rooms, so that would help you to overcome the problem you have with your current TV when it's sat next to your window.

'*The Q800 also comes with a free soundbar, so you wouldn't have to buy one separately, which means you'd get both within your budget.*

'*It also comes with free delivery and installation, so if you wanted to go with that today we could get it installed ready for the weekend, which would be great for when you have everyone round to watch the big game on Sunday.*

'*How does that sound?*'

Why even simple FAB presentations work

This process of starting with a clear proposal, and then presenting its key features, advantages and benefits as a series of cycles separated by short pauses, works well for a number of reasons.

1. **It positions you as a sales consultant.** In the medical world, a doctor diagnoses and prescribes across a very wide range of situations, whereas a consultant is a senior doctor who specializes in a particular field. A good salesperson can diagnose and prescribe a solution. A greater sales *consultant* does something similar, but with a greater degree of expertise.

2. **It ensures that your presentation is personalized.** Before you got to the presentation step of your conversation, you spent time talking with your customer – asking questions, actively listening to their answers and probing more deeply to ensure you have a good understanding of their needs. If you then move on to

deliver the same sales presentation you give to every customer, you'll throw all of the benefit of that understanding step out the window. Worse still, you risk alienating the customer, as they'll wonder why you bothered asking all those questions in the first place if you weren't ever going to do anything with the information they shared.

3. **It makes your presentations clear and easy to follow.** If you were to present multiple features all at once, and then go back to try to explain the advantages and benefits of each one, the link between each feature and why the customer should care about it is likely to get lost.

4. **It stops you from getting lost.** Not only do these short discrete FAB cycles make it easy for your customer to follow your presentation, delivering information in this way will help you to keep track of where you are too.

5. **It makes it easy to tell a story.** Humans love stories, and we tend to feel most comfortable and engage most readily with stories that follow a similar pattern – stories that start with a big picture introduction, then move onto the detail, and then end with a conclusion and perhaps what happens next. The approach of starting your presentation with your big recommendation, and then revealing its more detailed features, advantages and benefits, before finishing with a trial close, is consistent with the arc of a good story – big picture first, then the detail, then the conclusion and next steps at the end.

6. **It helps you to make justified recommendations.** This format of linking features and advantages directly to personalized benefits enables you to turn almost any feature into a mini-recommendation with its own justification built-in.

7. **It helps you to speak the customer's language.** Repeating words back to a customer that you heard them say during the understanding step of your conversation makes your justification even more powerful. It shows you were listening, and that what you're proposing is built around their needs. It's also highly influential, because essentially you're asking the customer to agree with themselves.

8. **It helps you to check and reinforce understanding.** The slight pause between each of your FAB cycles enables you to check and ensure that your customer understands, and is buying into what you're saying, as you go along. Even a brief pause of less than a second will give your customer the opportunity to jump in and ask a question, without feeling like they're interrupting. They also give you the opportunity to check in and ask a question if you pick-up on any confusion or unease from their body language too.

9. **It helps you to make your presentation interactive.** Just as you might pause to check for understanding, these pause points make natural opportunities for other types of interaction too. They can be ideal moments to introduce sales aids or props, or use other interaction techniques to expand on and reinforce the feature, advantage and benefit you've just explained.

10. **It makes it feel like a conversation.** The presenting step of your sales conversation is probably the step where both you and your customer expect you to be doing most of the talking. But your presentation shouldn't be a monologue or a speech. These cycles and pauses will help you to ensure you're talking *with*, and not *at*, your customer.

11. **It's short and to the point.** As you hopefully saw through the examples I shared, this model can enable you to deliver a clear and compelling sales presentation in just a few sentences. So even if you do have sales aids, props or other interactive tools you want to get your customer's hands on, it allows you to quickly get your main points across before you introduce anything that might otherwise distract from the key points of your presentation.

12. **It allows you to look for and quickly react to buying signals.** Just as the pause points provide great opportunities to check for understanding and introduce additional interaction, they give you the opportunity to check for buying signals too. Buying signals are verbal or non-verbal cues that show a customer is probably ready to buy what you're selling. If you see any, these pause points allow you to react, end the presentation there, and move immediately to close if you think the time's right – without it feeling as though you've jumped out of your presentation part way through to do so.

Building on your simple sales presentation

For many short-chain sales conversations, a simple FAB presentation – like the previous examples – is all you'll need. An active proposal for what the customer should do, justified by a short, personalized presentation.

But what if you feel your customer wants or is expecting more? If you're preparing for a more formal presentation, one you plan and rehearse in advance ready to present to a specific customer at a pre-arranged time, you may feel that such a short presentation feels a little inadequate. Your presentation may be over too quickly, especially if your customer has specifically put aside time to hear what you've got to say.

Or what if you feel there's more you need to discuss, share or demonstrate, before the customer would have sufficient information to make a properly informed buying decision?

In these situations you have two options:

1. use sales aids, case studies or other interaction tools to reinforce and build on the points you've already made; or

2. extend your presentation by adding more features, advantages and benefits into the mix.

Option 1 is often a great idea. Option 2 needs to be approached with care.

The dangers of feature overload

One danger of simply loading in more features is that your presentation can become confusing. Rather than improving things by giving the customer even more reasons to say yes, introducing more FAB cycles can actually make it more difficult for them to make a decision by invoking the paradox of choice.

In his 2004 book *The Paradox of Choice: Why More is Less*, psychologist Barry Schwartz explains that the paradox of choice is a psychological phenomenon that explains why, when we have more options to choose from, not only do we tend to find the decision-making process more difficult, but we're also less likely to be satisfied with any final decision we make.

So by presenting more features, although you might not think you've increased the number of options your customer has to choose from (you're still only presenting one solution after all), that isn't what it feels like from a decision-making point of view.

As humans we like to pin decisions on a single deciding factor, and adding more features, advantages and benefits into the mix gives the customer a much wider array of options to consider when they try to do that.

Another danger of adding more features into your presentation is that by doing so you might introduce a factor that the customer hasn't considered. The further you stray from the reasons you originally identified as justifying why *this* product or service is the best fit for the customer, the more likely you are to introduce something that will derail the deal, or cause your customer to delay making a decision while they take time to think through this new information.

So if you do decide to expand and build-out your sales presentation, be sure to do so without losing focus on the three to five key features you initially selected as being the most important. Instead, share additional information that aligns with these key features, helping to further justify your proposed solution, without making their decision more complex to think through.

When to introduce additional tools or information

As I pointed out earlier, one of the benefits of the FAB presentation structure is that the pause points between FAB cycles can make natural opportunities for you to introduce sales aids, props or other interactive tools. This approach is OK, as long as you're confident that what you introduce will help to build on the point you've just made, and that you won't get distracted, or forget to present the other FAB cycles you had planned.

The alternative approach is to quickly cover all the points you want to make by delivering a short and punchy FAB presentation like the examples I shared earlier, and *then* bridge to your additional sales aids, props or tools using phrases like these:

▶ *'Let me walk you through how that would work for you…';*

▶ *'Let me show you what I think that would do for your sales figures…'; or*

▶ *'Why don't you try it out for yourself…'*

Delivering sales presentations and demos is an area where there's lots you can learn and lots you can do to make them engaging, effective and enjoyable for your clients. But great sales presentations always have three to five clearly articulated FAB cycles at their heart.

What's next?

Once you've presented your recommended solution to your customer you'll probably be eager to try to close the sale. But before you do, it's important to test the water to see if your customer is actually ready to buy into what you've proposed. So that's what I'll show you how to do next.

Step 5
Trial close

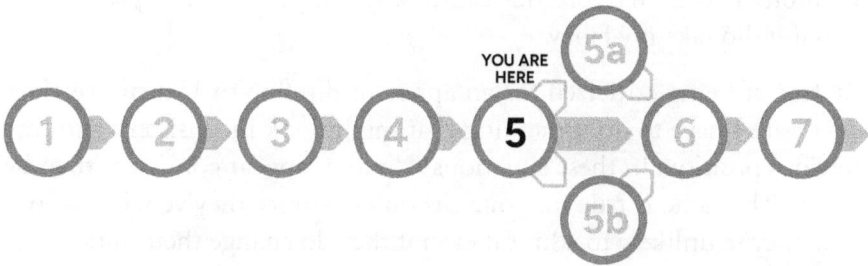

Figure 16: The New 7-Step Sale – Step 5

How to use a trial close

As I touched on in the previous chapter, it's important that you move to close the sale as soon as the customer is ready. Fail to do so, and you risk damaging your chances of closing as the prospect's level of engagement starts to drop. Worse still, you risk introducing something your prospect hasn't thought about, which leads to them back-pedalling from their mental buying decision while they consider this new information.

However, it's also important not to act too quickly. If you attempt to close a sale before a customer is ready, you run the risk of getting a 'no', which means you'll then have two hurdles to overcome: (1) you'll need to influence and persuade them to change their mind; and (2) you'll need to get them to admit that their initial buying decision was wrong.

The problem is that while the first is possible (after all, salespeople are experts at influencing and persuading people), the second can be much harder to do.

As you've already learnt in Chapter 2, one of the secrets to building and maintaining trust is to remain consistent. People naturally value consistency, not just in others, but also in themselves. Once we commit to something publicly we feel pressure to stick with it, even when our views change. The fear of looking inconsistent often outweighs any desire we have to do something differently.

I have personal experience of this. Five years ago I switched to a plant-based diet after reading about how it can extend and transform your quality of life. Something I try not to preach about, but will happily discuss, as it's something I've seen real benefits from. Does that mean I think I should never eat meat again? No! But it does mean that in most situations I wouldn't consider eating anything that wasn't plant-based, even if it did take my fancy.

My fear of being criticized for an apparent flip-flop or U-turn overrides any desire I have to do something that might look inconsistent with my previous position. In these situations I'd rather appear consistent than be honest. The same is true for your customers – once they've said 'No' out loud, they're unlikely to admit it even if they do change their mind.

But at some point you *do* have to ask the customer directly for their agreement to your proposal; you can't just wait until it's offered out of fear they'll say 'No' if you ask. But while their body language might give you a clue as to when they're ready for you to pop the question, there is a better way, and that's to use a trial close.

> *A trial close is an open-ended question that tells you where the customer is on their buying decision journey, and where you should go next within your 7-step sale.*

For example: *'How does that sound?'* or, *'What do you think?'*

Whatever you choose to ask, it's *very* important that your trial close is an open-ended question. Even if you aren't asking a question that's directly linked to the final buying decision, now is not the time to risk putting the word 'no' into the buyer's mind or, even worse, into their mouth.

It's also important not to confuse a trial close with other, less ethical, closing techniques. I'll cover ethical versus unethical closing in 'Step 6: Close the sale'. For now, simply know that not only is a question like 'when would you like to go ahead?' not a trial close, the manipulative assumption embedded within it also means it's not a closing technique you should use either.

When to drop-in a trial close

If you stick with a broad, open-ended question, then a trial close is a valuable technique that you can use in many situations. For example, you can drop-in a trial close:

▶ at almost any time after you've started your presentation and outlined your recommended solution;

▶ in the deliberate pauses you make between FAB cycles to check how your presentation is being received;

▶ if you get lost in the flow of your presentation and want a moment to re-establish where you are; or

▶ whenever you think you see the customer displaying buying signals, to check if your reading of the situation is correct, *before* you move to close.

Trial close responses and next steps

A trial close is a great way of testing the water. Not only can it help you to find out where the customer is on their buying decision journey, but it also helps you to understand where you should lead the conversation next.

Unlike a closed-ended question, using an open-ended trial close doesn't risk painting yourself into a corner you can't easily get out of. Broad-natured and open-ended trial close questions, like 'How does that sound?' or 'What do you think?', allow you to naturally continue the sales conversation no matter what answer you receive in response.

Each response you receive to your trial close will fall into one of four categories, and each one gives you a clear direction for where you should lead the conversation next. If you refer back to Figure 8 from the chapter introducing the New 7-Step Sale, you can see the potential next steps represented by the four different arrows leading from the trial close, either looping back to presenting, or moving forward to overcome objections, negotiate, or close.

Let's examine each of these options in more detail.

How to respond to buying signals

When you ask a trial close question, you're likely hoping that your customer will respond with a phrase like 'that sounds great', giving you a clear signal that they're probably ready to buy. When this happens, you need to avoid the temptation to carry on presenting, and move immediately to close the sale. (I'll show you how you can do that almost effortlessly in Step 6.)

The possibility, if not the probability of a 'that sounds great' response, helps to explain why the overcome objections and negotiate steps sit off to the side of the main pathway in the New 7-Step Sale diagram as shown in Figure 8 in the introduction to this part of the book. While you should be ready to handle and overcome objections or negotiate if necessary, it's a mistake to assume that you'll need to do either. Your objective is to plan and prepare effectively, and then engage and understand the customer's individual needs, so that when you present your personalized solution, they accept it without you having to further justify it or adapt it in any way.

Your objective is to: *Prepare, Engage, Present, Trial Close, Close and Follow-up – without having to handle objections or negotiate at all if possible.*

How to respond to questions

The second type of response you may get to your trial close is that the customer might ask a question. For example, they might ask you to recap or expand on something from your presentation, or they might ask for some information about an aspect of your solution you haven't yet explained. In either case, this shows that they're probably not ready to make a buying decision yet.

Many salespeople confuse questions asked at this stage of the conversation with objections. For example, they believe that because the customer asked a question to clarify the price, it means they're not happy with the price quoted. Don't make this mistake. Don't make assumptions about what a customer is thinking, and respond by putting thoughts into their head or words into their mouth that might not have been there.

Questions about price, contracts, payment terms and so on are often positive buying signals, where the customer is simply confirming they understand something important before they're ready to commit. So your response to these types of questions, or in fact to any question your customers pose at this stage of your conversation, should simply be to loop back to the presentation step and answer the question they asked, and not the objection you fear might be lurking beneath it.

Once you've done that, and have answered any follow-up questions they might have, move on to test the water once again by asking another trial close question, such as 'So, what do you think?' If there *was* an objection lurking beneath their question, this second trial close will probably draw it out. I'll explain how to handle and overcome objections shortly, but first, let's address another type of response that you might fear your trial close could lead to.

What about rejections?

In the context of closing the sale, a rejection is a firm, clear and unambiguous 'no' to your proposal or recommendation.

For the reasons I've already covered, once you've received a rejection from your customer, it can be difficult (but not impossible), for you to recover and successfully close the sale. I'll explain how to deal with rejections in more detail in Step 6. But for now, the good news is that if you delivered your trial close correctly, by asking a broad *open-ended* question, it's unlikely you'll receive an outright rejection in response.

This is another reason why the trial close is such a powerful sales technique and an important step in the New 7-Step Sale, because you can ask it without fear of rejection. You can drop-in a trial close at almost any point, safe in the knowledge that the response will give you guidance on where to go next, without the risk that you'll derail your sales conversation.

How to respond to a negotiation request

In some cases, customers might respond to your trial close question by trying to negotiate a better deal. This could be a direct request which might sound something like 'If you can [do x], then we have a deal', or it could be an indirect request which might sound more like 'Can you do this for a lower price?'

In these situations, if what they're asking for is, (1) reasonable, and (2) something you can concede without significantly reducing the value you'll receive in return, then you might be tempted to agree. But be careful. Agree too quickly, and this first request for you to compromise might not be their last.

When a customer tries to negotiate you should see this as a good sign, because it's a clear buying signal. They might not be ready to buy yet, but they're indicating that's where they'd like to get to. Here are four ways you can respond if a customer tries to negotiate with you at this stage of your conversation.

▶ **Option 1: Stand your ground.** If you choose this response, your objective is to stand your ground without drawing a line in the sand that you couldn't cross later if you chose to do so. So avoid giving a reflex response that might rule out negotiating later, such as 'This is the best I could do', which might prompt the customer to call your bluff and end the sales conversation there.

However, in these situations you're perfectly within your rights to be firm and put the ball back in their court. To do that, the first thing you need to do is to pause. Not only does this give you time to think, but if their attempt to negotiate wasn't serious and was just a 'try on' or a 'cheeky request', you may find they step in to fill the silence and talk themselves out of it. If they don't, try standing your ground using a non-committal phrase like 'I think what we've discussed is a good deal', and then shut-up and wait for them to respond. You may find that's all it takes for them to back down and accept your initial proposal. If standing your ground in this way doesn't work, it still leaves your options open so you can move on to one of the other approaches below.

▶ **Option 2: Treat it as an objection.** An attempt to negotiate is a request for you to compromise by changing your proposal so that it's more favourable to the customer – and usually less favourable to you as a result. However, you don't want to do that unless you absolutely have to. One way to reduce the chances you'll have to go down that path later, is to handle the request as if it's an objection you can help the customer overcome, instead of changing your position to remove what may only be a perceived hurdle rather than a real barrier. I'll explain how to handle and overcome objections in the next chapter.

▶ **Option 3: Isolate, trade and agree.** If what the customer has asked for is something you'd be happy to agree to in order to close the sale, the first thing you need to do is to confirm the request they've made for you to compromise is an isolated example that won't be followed by further requests if you agree. You can do that by asking a question such as 'Is there anything else you'd like to review?' If this question reveals there are other things they'd like to address, then this quick 'isolate, trade and agree' approach isn't the best way forward.

However, even if you are able to isolate that what they're asking for is the only change they'd like you to make, in a negotiation you should never give anything away for free. So you need to follow that with a question like 'If I can find a way to do that, can we finalize the deal here and now?' This is your trade. If you *are* going to compromise, then you at least need to trade that for their immediate and binding agreement in return.

Only when you've isolated that this is the only compromise they want you to make, and they've confirmed they're happy to trade that for their immediate acceptance to all other aspects of your proposal, should you agree to their counteroffer and move forward to close the sale.

▶ **Option 4: Open a negotiation.** The final option for how you can respond to a request for you to compromise or change your proposed solution, is to move to the negotiation step of the New 7-Step Sale. The 'isolate, trade and agree' response outlined in Option 3 *is* actually a mini-negotiation. However, if you discover there's more than one area they want you to compromise on, or if what they're requesting isn't fair or isn't something you'd want to agree to without asking for additional compromises from their side, then you're going to need a more considered approach to your negotiation. I'll explain how to do that in more detail in the chapter 'Step 5b: Negotiate'.

How to respond to objections

The final type of response you might receive to your trial close is for the customer to raise an objection.

An objection isn't a 'no', nor is it when a customer asks for something extra in return for their agreement. An objection is when a customer responds by sharing a reason why they're not happy with what you've proposed, by saying something like *'I'm not sure about…'* or *'I'm not a big fan of…'*

Handling and overcoming objections takes skill. I'll show you how to do that in the next chapter.

What's next?

As you've just learnt, the trial close is a pivot point in your sales conversation – the answer you receive to your trial close question can lead you in a number of different directions. Although I hope your trial close will draw out clear buying signals indicating your customer *is* ready for you to close, trial closes are also good at drawing out objections. So that's what we'll deal with next.

Step 5a
Handle and overcome objections

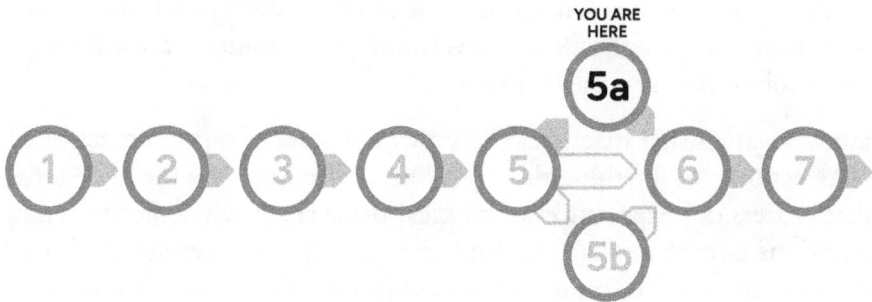

Figure 17: The New 7-Step Sale – Step 5a

Why objections (and rejections) hurt

Even if you're selling a competitively priced product or service that solves significant problems your customers' face, *and* you follow the New 7-Step Sale with skill and mastery, you're still going to receive both objections and rejections. It's just a fact of life.

As I explained in the previous chapter, rejections and objections aren't the same. A *rejection* is a clear and unambiguous refusal by your customer to accept the solution you've proposed – it's a firm '*no*' – whereas an *objection* is a specific reason why a customer isn't happy to move forward – it's a *'not yet, because…'*

But although rejections and objections are different, many salespeople confuse them because they *feel* very similar.

In order to get to this point in your sales conversation, you first spent time planning and preparing; then you successfully engaged the customer in conversation and asked carefully crafted questions to understand their needs and wants; then you moved on to propose a solution that you're confident would be good for both of you, which you justified and explained by delivering a personalized presentation.

In short, you invested a lot to get to this point, so it's understandable you're going to be disappointed when a customer tells you they're not happy to move forward.

But it's worse than that, because every time you face a rejection or an objection, it's going to *physically* hurt. The knowledge that you did everything right isn't going to stop that happening, and preparing yourself for the certainty that you're going to face them at some point won't make them hurt any less either. Rejections and objections hurt because humans have evolved to *ensure* they do.

Studies using fMRI machines show that the areas of our brain activated by rejection – or anything that feels like a rejection – are the same areas that process our experiences of physical pain. That's why objections and rejections hurt more than we think they should, because they don't just damage our ego, they cause us real pain too. So why are our brains wired that way?

Humans are social creatures. One of the reasons we've been highly successful as a species for more than 200,000 years is because we live in cooperative and collaborative groups. Our evolutionary ancestors who lived in large social groups were more likely to be successful at hunting and gathering food, fighting off attackers and bringing up young, than their more solitary cousins. So the genes and biological processes that evolved to make our ancestors feel bad if they did anything that led to rejection by their peers were passed down because they're a survival advantage – don't get thrown out of the cave!

This is why not only do rejections hurt, but anything that feels like it might lead to a rejection makes us feel bad too. Our fear of rejection evolved because it helps to dissuade us from taking actions that might lead to us being rejected in future.

The techniques in this book will help you to minimize the chance that you'll receive an objection, maximize the chance that you'll be able to overcome one when it does arise, and reduce how much and for how long any rejections you *are* faced with will hurt. But you can't stop rejections from hurting altogether, and fear of rejection is perfectly natural too. No matter what anyone says, we all suffer from it.

This is yet another reason why the trial close technique from the previous chapter is so powerful, because you can use it without fear that it could lead directly to a rejection. As you'll see when you get to 'Step 6: Close the sale', the trial close can also help to make that important step much easier and less fear-inducing too. But as it's inevitable you're going to have to handle and overcome objections at some point, here's how to do that.

Handling vs overcoming objections

Once you're faced with an objection, you're going to need to handle and overcome it before you can move forward. If you read around this subject, you'll often see the terms *handle* and *overcome* used interchangeably, but they're not the same.

Think of handling objections as how you respond. *Handling* describes the general approach you take, the framework you work within, and the process you follow.

Overcoming *objections* (or, as I prefer to think of it, helping the customer to overcome *their* objections – because you can't do it for them) is just one step within the broader handling process. But it shouldn't be the first step, as if the first thing you do is try to overcome the objection, then at best you're likely to come across as defensive and at worst customers will feel you're trying to push them in a particular direction, and that can trigger their reactance.

Reactance is a psychological response that can occur when we feel we're being pressured to do something that's contrary to our values, needs or wants. Not only can reactance cause someone to adopt or strengthen a position that's opposite to the pressure they're feeling, but it can also increase their resistance to any attempt to persuade them otherwise.

Triggering a customer's reactance is not good, because not only will it make your job harder, but it can also cause you to get pulled into a discussion that can quickly escalate into a heated debate or, worse still, into a full-blown argument.

So it's important that you handle the objection correctly *before* you try to help the customer overcome it.

If you read around this subject you'll find many different objection-handling frameworks, and some sales leaders propose using different techniques in different situations. However, if you have a variety of frameworks and approaches to choose from, in the heat of the moment it can be easy to get confused. The emotionally charged step of objection handling is a part of your sales conversation where sticking to a single process will serve you well.

The 'magic' solution?

I'm sorry to be the bearer of bad news, but there is no magic solution. A good objection handling process *will* increase the chance you'll be able to help your customer to overcome their objection, but it won't guarantee it.

The truth is that just like every other salesperson on the planet, you *will* meet objections that you can't get past and, as a result, you *will* face rejections from time to time. It's a fact of life. Be very wary of anybody who tells you otherwise.

However, there is a process that's suitable for any type of objection you might face that's proven to maximize your chances of overcoming it. Here it is.

AEIO objection handling

The stages in the AEIO objection-handling process, are:

1. Accept

2. Explore

3. Isolate

4. Overcome

Figure 18: The AEIO objection-handling process

Stage 1: Accept

You know that the last thing you should do when faced with an objection is to push back, because doing so could trigger the customer's reactance. This would not only cause the customer to strengthen their position in opposition to your proposal, but it would also make them more resistant to any attempt you might make to persuade them otherwise.

However, rather than fearing objections, you need to learn to embrace them – because they're a natural part of the decision-making process. Whenever we make a considered decision, we're usually weighing up the pros and cons, and when a customer's happy to let you in on their decision-making process, that's a demonstration of trust. It also indicates they're open to discussion, and so you should see this as an active invitation to help them overcome the obstacles standing in the way of the win-win outcome that would benefit you both.

So you mustn't push back against objections, but you should do more than just mentally accept them – you've got to actively demonstrate your acceptance of them to the customer too.

Customers are used to salespeople. They know what often happens when they raise an objection, and so at this stage they'll be hypersensitive to anything that might even vaguely look like a manipulative tactic. A simple neutral acceptance of their position isn't going to persuade them that an attempt to manipulate isn't still coming. What you need to do instead is to surprise them (nicely), by moving *with* them – and to do that you need to use a bit of sales judo.

Judo, which means 'gentle way', is a Japanese martial art that makes use of an opponent's weight and momentum. In judo, instead of resisting when your opponent pushes you, one technique is to offer no resistance to put them off balance. You can even enhance the effect by increasing your speed of movement in the same direction while pulling them with you.

So, rather than pushing back, you actively move with them. The effect is like them going to push on a sticking door, only to find that you're pulling it open from the other side.

In the context of a sales objection this can be a nice surprise for the customer. Rather than getting the resistance they expected, they find you're acknowledging and accepting their objection, or even actively agreeing with it.

So what does this look like in a sales context?

Even if you don't agree with a customer's objection (for example, perhaps you believe it's factually wrong), you can still accept and acknowledge it in a positive way by using phrases such as:

> ▶ *'That's a good point'*;
>
> ▶ *'I get it. I've heard that from other customers too'*;
>
> ▶ *'I can't argue with that'*; or
>
> ▶ *'That's a valid concern, and one I think I'd have in your situation'.*

If what they're saying is correct (and, if they're expressing their *opinion*, it can't be wrong), then you can go further and actively move in the same direction by using phrases such as:

> ▶ *'I agree'*;
>
> ▶ *'You're right'*; or
>
> ▶ *'That's exactly how I feel'.*

Whatever response you choose, you must be seen to move positively *with* them.

As well as avoiding negative responses, you should try to avoid non-committal phrases such as 'OK' or 'I understand' too. While these don't necessarily demonstrate resistance, customers may take them as an indicator that resistance is coming, or at least that it's potentially hidden in the background.

You also need to avoid any responses that might sound condescending, so don't do or say anything at this point that could indicate you feel the customer's objection comes from their ignorance or misunderstanding. Even if that might be true, that would be *your* fault, not theirs. You either didn't ask the right questions at the understanding stage, didn't listen effectively to the responses you received, didn't present the right information, or didn't explain it in the right way. Show empathy by mentally putting yourself in their shoes, not sympathy by demonstrating your pity for their misfortune.

Stage 2: Explore

Once you've positively accepted the customer's objection, the next stage is to explore it to ensure you both understand it fully. Your task is to make the objection as specific as possible and ensure you understand its root cause.

This is important, because you need to be confident you're about to help the customer overcome their *actual* objection, rather than spending time chasing your incorrect assumption, or, worse still, create another objection that didn't exist until you put words into the customer's mouth.

To do this, you're going to work *with* the customer, and explore the objection together using your questioning skills from the understanding step of your sales conversation, by asking:

▷ open-ended questions, such as 'Who...?', 'What...?', 'Where...?', 'When...?', 'Which...?' and 'How...?';

▷ probing questions, such as 'Tell me...', 'Explain to me...', and 'Describe for me...'; and

▷ closed-ended clarification questions, such as 'Am I right in thinking...?'

When handling an objection, it's particularly important for you to phrase your questions carefully for two reasons.

First, you need to ensure your customer is clear that you're asking questions purely to gain a deeper understanding, and that you're not questioning their ability or opinion. If you got the 'Accept' stage of the handling process right, you've already started to pull the customer towards you, so be careful not to push them away again during your exploration.

One way to do this is to avoid asking any question that starts with the word 'Why...?'. 'Why...?' questions, can come across as though you're questioning the customer's judgement, rather than trying to find out about what led to a particular situation. They can also trigger customers to give an emotional or defensive response, which is not what you want.

So try to ask 'What…?' questions instead, as these are likely to give you the more rational and considered answers you're looking for.

Second, as your customer is likely to be hypersensitive to anything that might indicate or be construed as manipulation at this stage, now is *not* the time to ask leading questions either. Your goal is to help the customer overcome their objection, not to try to do that for them. If they think your questions are designed to lead them in a particular direction, you're likely to trigger their reactance.

Here are some examples of exploration questions you might ask.

- ▶ *'When you say we're too expensive, what does that mean?'*

- ▶ *'I agree that our service is a significant investment; what sort of return would we need to deliver to make that worth your while?'*

- ▶ *'Budget wise, what else are we competing with?'*

- ▶ *'When you speak with your partner, which aspects of our solution do you think they'll want to focus on?'*

- ▶ *'What aspects do I need to work on to compete against your existing provider more effectively?'*

- ▶ *'Which aspects in particular are you unsure of?'*

- ▶ *'Which aspects of the contract concern you specifically?'*

Just as it was during the understanding step of your conversation, it's very important that you listen closely and actively to the responses you receive. This is often more difficult when handling objections, because the process is typically more complex, more emotional, and requires more actively thought-through and carefully worded questions and responses.

So as you ask your exploration questions, one tip is to move more slowly than you did during the understanding step of your conversation. Don't be afraid of thoughtful pauses. Not only will this help you to keep your defensive instincts in check, it will also give you time to carefully consider how you'll phrase your questions and responses. The silence can also encourage your customer to fill the gaps and provide more useful information, and sometimes you'll find that customers overcome their own objections in the process!

Stage 3: Isolate

Once you're sure that you both understand the objection and its root cause, the next stage is to isolate it by checking whether there are any other objections you'll need to deal with. This is important because at this stage you don't know whether the objection you're faced with is the customer's only objection, or even if it's their most significant concern.

The process of isolating an objection also helps to reveal whether you've been handling a real objection or a red herring, and whether there are other hidden objections lurking in the background that are yet to be revealed. You don't want to spend time helping the customer to overcome an objection only to have another thrown at you afterwards.

Here are two examples of isolation questions you might ask.

▶ *'Other than this, is there anything else that's concerning you?'*; or

▶ *'Is there anything else that could stop us moving forward?'*

If your isolation question reveals that further objections *do* exist, then before you move forward it's important that you also explore each of them in turn, just as you did with the first objection they raised. In situations where you're facing multiple objections, I recommend that once you've explored each one, you write it down. Then, when you've explored all of the customer's objections, ask another isolation question so that you can be sure you've uncovered everything that's preventing you moving forward.

Creating a bullet-point list of all of the customer's objections is a powerful tool. It shows the customer that you're taking their concerns seriously, it will give you a structure to follow that will help you to lead and retain control of the conversation moving forward, and it will help as you ask the following important question:

▶ *'So, if we can find a way of satisfying this concern, [or all of these concerns], would you be happy to move forward?'*

If the customer answers 'No' to that question, what would that tell you? It would indicate that there's at least one other hidden objection you need to uncover, and you can do so simply by asking another isolation question:

▶ *'OK, what else do we need to resolve?'*

If the customer answers 'Yes', then what have they just done? They've potentially pre-closed the sale for you! If you can find a way of satisfying all of their objections, then they've effectively just said 'yes' to your proposal. Of course, you'll be sure to go back and confirm this with an effective close at the appropriate time, but at that stage you can almost treat the close as a formality.

If you had more than one objection on your list, then there's a final question you now need to ask:

▶ *'Where shall we start? Which of these is your biggest concern?'*

You don't want to spend time working through minor objections to find you're still left with a larger problem you can't overcome, so asking a question like that will help you to prioritize.

Stage 4: Overcome

In order to get to this stage of the objection-handling process, you've: accepted the customer's objection and pulled the customer towards you; explored the objection to ensure you understand it correctly; and isolated the objection to make sure there aren't any others you'll have to deal with, or if there are, prioritized them to ensure you're going to handle the biggest one first. Now it's time to help the customer overcome their objection, so you can move forward with the win-win solution you've proposed.

As with all of the techniques I present in this book, I want you to make the task of overcoming objections your own, by injecting a bit of your own personality and adapting to your customers. But before I give you the technique I recommend you use as a base, here are the principles you need to adhere to.

▶ **Principle 1: Relate.** Continue to pull the customer towards you by showing your gratitude, and that you can relate to what they're telling you. This is about demonstrating empathy not sympathy, so avoid using phrases such as *'I'm sorry you feel that way'*. Instead, use phrases such as: *'Thank you for sharing that'*; *'That's actually something I hear a lot from other customers'*; *'I'd have exactly the same concern in your situation'*; or *'I get why this is an issue for you and I think I can help'*.

▶ **Principle 2: Compensate.** The key to compensating is to provide new information that specifically relates to the objection in hand.

Don't try to compensate by presenting more unrelated features in the hope that their advantages and benefits will outweigh this particular concern. Also, you mustn't just repeat something you told them earlier in your conversation, as doing so would be akin to saying: *'I've told you this before, so you're either stupid or you just weren't listening.'*

Often, the best new information to share at this stage isn't *your* words, it's those of others. When people are struggling to make a decision, they often look for social proof from others to help them – and the more connected they feel with those others, the more influential this proof becomes. Two ways of doing this can be by sharing case studies about customers like them who overcame similar concerns with successful results, or by sharing independent reviews. This is where your planning and preparation comes in, as if you know the objections you're likely to face (perhaps those you face regularly from similar customers), then you can have this social proof primed and ready.

All of this helps to demonstrate why it's often best to keep your initial sales presentation short, by holding detailed information and case studies back, ready to share them as part of your objection handling should you need to.

▷ **Principle 3: Demonstrate.** Part of the problem with helping a customer to overcome any objection is the status quo bias – the emotional preference we all have for the current state of affairs, which we explored in Chapter 4. With this bias, the current situation (or status quo) is taken as a reference point, and any change from that is underpinned by a fear of loss. Put another way, it's 'better the devil you know than the devil you don't' type thinking.

To overcome this, you're going to need to demonstrate the value your customer will receive if they change their position. As well as highlighting the *benefits* of your solution, you can also demonstrate this by highlighting what they'll lose if they *don't* change. This is because fear of loss is often a more compelling reason to change than a desire to gain.

Once again, you need to ensure you do this by providing new information, not by repeating or rephrasing things you've already said. So help them to paint a mental picture of the value they'll gain by changing, and what they'll lose if they don't.

How to overcome objections using a 'feel, felt, found' case study

A simple way to help a customer overcome their objections in a way that relates, compensates and demonstrates value, is to use the 'feel, felt, found' technique. Although widely used, this technique was first proposed by Zig Ziglar in his 1982 book, *Zig Ziglar's Secrets of Closing the Sale*. The three elements of this technique are:

1. **feel** – acknowledge the customer's concern;

2. **felt** – relate the customer's concern to a similar concern expressed by a different customer; and

3. **found** – explain how the other customer overcame their concern, and benefited from using your product or service as a result.

The easiest way to cover all three of these elements is through a simple case study about another customer – one who is similar to the customer you're speaking with and had the same reservations, but managed to overcome them with great success.

Here are some examples of what a mini 'feel, felt, found' case study might sound like.

▶ *'I understand why you might feel that way. Mr Smith, another customer of mine, felt that way too, but what he found was...'*

▶ *'I understand why you might feel the price is too high. Other customers have felt the same way too, but when they saw the efficiency savings, they found it was a really good investment. Let me walk you through an example...'*

▶ *'I understand how you feel about the price; many of our clients have felt the same way too. This is why we offer a 30-day price match guarantee to give all our clients peace of mind, but we've found that customers aren't able to find a better deal elsewhere'.*

▶ *'I understand why you feel nervous about switching; I've had many customers who felt the same way too, but they find that because of the support we provide, the disruption they feared just doesn't happen. Here's what I'll do to ensure you have the same experience...'*

Once you've shared your 'feel, felt, found' case study, what do you think you should do to test the water to see whether your customer is now ready to buy? You should simply drop back to the previous step in the New 7-Step Sale, and ask another trial close question. What do you think?

What's next?

If you've successfully helped your customer to overcome their objections, and perhaps dropped in another trial close to make sure, your next step would be to move forward and close the sale. But what about when your objection handling fails? In these cases, rather than walking away, another option is to negotiate a compromised solution – one that's different from your original proposal, but still represents a win-win outcome. So let's move on to look at how to do that.

Step 5b
Negotiate

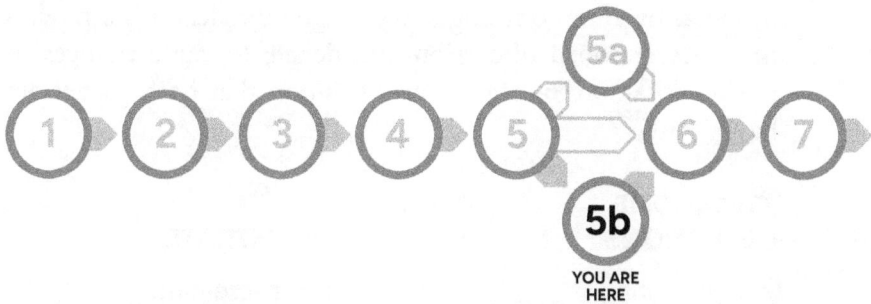

Figure 19: The New 7-Step Sale – Step 5b

Negotiating vs overcoming objections

Selling can involve both influence and persuasion. However, these are two slightly different actions.

▶ *Influencing* is about using knowledge, skill and credibility to affect another person's opinions or actions. A good salesperson uses influence throughout the entire sales conversation.

▶ *Persuasion* involves using reasoned discussion and debate, to openly encourage another person to change what they believe or do.

So, the *overcome objections* and *negotiate steps* of your sales conversation mark the points where you'll move from influencing into persuading. In fact, a good way to think of negotiation is that it's a structured form of persuasion you can use when required – but, just like handling objections, it isn't a step that necessarily forms part of every sales conversation.

But although the *overcome objections* and *negotiate steps* are similar, they're not the same.

▶ *Overcoming objections* involves helping the customer to reassess their initial dissatisfaction with your proposal, by persuading them that there's already sufficient value in the solution you've presented to justify the price you're asking. It involves using reasoned discussion and debate to change the customer's mind, *without* changing the deal.

▶ *Negotiating* is the act of overcoming objections to your initial proposal by compromising and *changing* the deal. It's a process that uses reasoned discussion and debate to agree changes to the proposal, or co-create a new solution that both parties are happy with.

OVERCOME OBJECTIONS
by highlighting existing common ground

NEGOTIATE
by co-creating new common ground

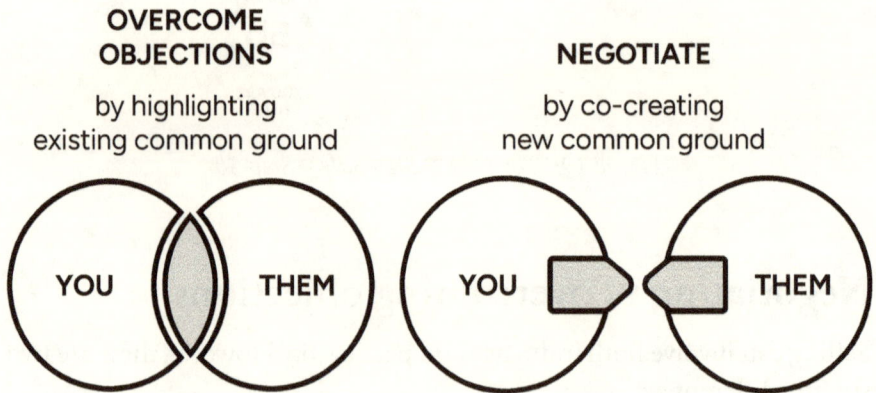

YOU   THEM   YOU   THEM

Figure 20: Overcoming objections vs negotiation

When to negotiate

As with handling and overcoming objections, you shouldn't aim to negotiate. However, there are situations where negotiation can become necessary.

One example is when there's an imbalance of benefit. Negotiation often happens when *both* parties share a common interest or goal (for example, you have something to sell that your customer would like to buy), but *one* party believes the proposed deal is weighted too heavily in the other party's favour. So one way you can trigger a negotiation is by pitching too high, prompting your customer to directly ask for a better deal.

Another example of when negotiation can become necessary is if your objection handling fails. Whenever you're unable to persuade your customer to accept your proposed solution by handling and overcoming their objections, opening a negotiation becomes your alternative to just walking away.

There are other routes into a negotiation, but negotiation typically becomes necessary when one party feels hard done by. So the degree to which everyone trusts each other can be a major factor in determining whether a negotiation will be necessary or successful.

But the decision to open a negotiation isn't one you should take lightly. As we'll explore shortly, at its heart, negotiation is about trading – exchanging one thing for something else – an act that will likely involve you compromising on your preferred position.

While any deal you negotiate should still be fair, and should still represent a 'win' for both you and your customer, the return on investment you'll gain from a negotiated outcome is likely to be different from the one you originally envisaged. The final deal might be better, it might be worse, or it might just be different.

Alternatively, you might waste time, energy and other resources trying to negotiate a deal, without ever being able to reach an agreement you're both happy with. In this case you'd have been better off standing your ground, sticking with your original proposal and walking away to invest your time elsewhere.

So a negotiation isn't something you should rush into.

How to negotiate

Before I explain how to negotiate, I first want to add a little context. Negotiations can be incredibly complex, especially those where the term *negotiation* captures the perspective of how both parties see the entire conversation. That's often the case for certain stages of more complex long-chain sales, and in those instances 'how to negotiate' could be the title of a whole book, or even a series of books.

So what I'm going to share in this chapter is how to negotiate as part of an individual sales conversation. However, as with everything in this book, this method is based on core principles and fundamental skills that will serve you well throughout the whole of your sales career – even if you do move into enterprise-level sales at a later stage.

This process of negotiating mirrors the AEIO process for handling and overcoming objections. In fact, for a negotiation that's embedded within a 7-step sales conversation, the best place to start is to attempt to handle and overcome the objection so you don't have to negotiate a compromised deal at all.

Therefore, in a negotiation, you need to:

- **A: Accept** that it's perfectly natural that a customer might want to voice and discuss the potential 'cons' that they're balancing against the 'pros' of the solution you've proposed;

- **E: Explore** their concerns to ensure you both have a good understanding of what's causing the customers unease or dissatisfaction;.

- **I: Isolate** all the customer's concerns from the rest of your proposed solution, ensuring that you get everything that they're potentially unhappy about into the open; and

- **O:** if you can't **overcome** their objections by standing your ground and persuading the customer of the value of your proposed solution, you can then move to **open** a negotiation.

Moving from objection handling to opening a negotiation in this way not only feels like a natural next step if your attempts to overcome the objection fails, but also it puts you in a strong position from which to negotiate successfully – because, by this point, you'll have a clear understanding of what's currently preventing you from being able to move forward.

How to adopt and promote the right mindset

A great negotiator is able to balance the courage to protect their own interests with consideration for the other party's needs, while also minimizing the potential for any conflict if their counterpart isn't so fair minded, or just has a different opinion about what constitutes a 'fair' or successful outcome.

However, as well as managing this external balance and potential conflict, negotiators often have to manage a potential internal conflict too – one between their head and their heart.

For many salespeople, effective negotiation can feel counter-intuitive, because what our instincts and our rational brains tell us we should do when we're challenged often don't align. For this reason, it's critical to challenge your thinking and consciously shift your mindset before a negotiation even begins. Good negotiators use their head, not their heart, in negotiations.

A good way to adopt the right mindset is to view negotiation as collaboration, rather than confrontation. See the obstacles that stand between you and a successful outcome as joint problems for you and your customer to work on and overcome together as partners. Ensuring that you not only see a negotiation this way, but that you also describe it in similar terms, can help influence your customer to adopt a similar mindset.

The words you use can have a powerful impact on how any potential negotiation plays out further down the line. For example, participants in a study conducted by Stanford University behaved twice as cooperatively when a game was introduced as 'The Community Game', compared to 'The Wall Street Game'. So to avoid prompting your customer to behave competitively, don't describe it as a 'negotiation'. Instead, focus on words that depict cooperative and collaborative behaviour, such as 'action planning'.

You should also avoid words that indicate division or polarized viewpoints. Even simple words like 'mine' and 'yours', or 'accept' and 'reject', can cause people to behave more aggressively in a negotiation. Instead, focus on words that position you both as being on the same team, such as 'us' or 'we', and in the right context, 'our'. These words will help to emphasize your shared goal, and you'll usually be able to gain a more favourable deal as a result.

How to identify what you can (and can't) negotiate

Negotiation is not about getting your customer to back down, or to concede to your demands. At its heart, negotiation is about trading, exchanging one thing for something else. So to negotiate effectively, both sides *must be open* to changing their position in order to move forward.

I touched on this when I explained the 'isolate, trade and agree' process in the trial close responses section of Step 5, which is an example of a mini-negotiation in itself. There I explained that, even if you were happy to accept the counteroffer your customer put forward, in a negotiation you should never give anything away for free. Instead, I suggested you could trade your concession for their immediate and binding agreement. But what else could you trade?

Salespeople often believe that negotiations are all about price, or if they're unable to change the price of what they sell, that their ability to negotiate is hampered as a result. But this isn't true.

As I explained in Chapter 7, you're always selling a package made up of a number of elements, but you might also be able to receive a package of elements in return – one that includes more than just a financial payment.

These packages may include *tangibles* – elements you can see or touch – as well as *intangibles* – elements that have no physical form but still have value. It's only when all of these individual elements are identified and recognized that the true value of the package can be determined.

The 'headline' elements within a product or service package offered to a customer typically include:

- ▶ **specification** – what products or services will be included, and what support will be provided, and so on;

- ▶ **volume** – how many, how much, what types, etc.;

- ▶ **delivery** – when, where, how, lead times, response times, etc.;

- ▶ **price, fee or margin** – how much will be paid, and to whom;

- ▶ **payment terms** – when, how, and in what currency, etc.; and

- ▶ **contract period** – when it will start, how long it will run for, under what circumstances will it or can it be or terminated, and when will it be reviewed, etc.

But there can be many more elements too, which we'll come back to shortly.

All of the elements that can or can't be negotiated fall into one of two categories.

▶ **Fixed elements, or 'absolutes'.** These are the things you can't change, and so there's no scope for negotiation. For many salespeople, this will include elements such as the nature of the individual products or services themselves, as well as key terms such as the minimum order quantity or delivery schedule. For some salespeople, the prices of the products or services they sell may also be fixed.

▶ **Variable elements, or 'variables'.** These are the things you, or your customer, can agree to change in order to reach an agreement. They may include factors over which you have a lot of control – such as the level of advice, guidance and support you provide after the sale is agreed; factors over which you have some control, but may only vary within pre-determined limits – payment terms are often a good example of these; and factors where the only variable is whether it's included within the deal or not.

While the fixed elements will be important to recognize and discuss, it is, of course, around the variables that negotiation conversations revolve.

Many salespeople fail to consider variables that may seem peripheral or inconsequential to a sale, but which can become very important during a negotiation.

These variables could include things that either party could provide or withhold, cause or deny, or save or cost the other, where changing the variable would also change the perceived value of the deal. Here are some examples.

▶ **Time.** What could you do to save them time? And what could *they* do to save *you* time?

▶ **Effort.** What could you, or they, do to reduce the effort you each need to put in?

▶ **Information.** What information could you, or they, provide, that the other party would find valuable?

▶ **Advice and support.** Could you share your expertise, or provide support that would help them to achieve their objectives or goals? Could they do anything similar to help you to reach yours?

▶ **Personal satisfaction.** Could you do something that would help them to feel good about themselves?

▷ **External recognition.** Could you do something that would improve the way others see them? Could they do something similar for you – provide referrals or testimonials, for example?

Notice that in this list I focus on the positive impact you could have on each other. This is important. Effective negotiations focus on variables you could change to add value, improve ROI or help the other party to avoid pain. You should never try to negotiate using negative outcomes or threats.

How to consider cost vs value

Each element of your package has a value to your customer, but it also has a cost that you incur to provide it, and of course the same is true in reverse. However, the cost and value of each element is not necessarily linked. Here are some examples to demonstrate that.

▷ Sharing your expertise is of low cost to you – the only cost is usually just the time it takes for you to pass on your insights and recommendations, but your expertise may be hugely valuable to your customer. Often, providing a simple and seemingly innocuous piece of advice can be all it takes to enable your customer to save a significant amount of time, effort or money.

▷ If your organization has a large warehouse, a big delivery fleet and a stable and continuous supply of stock, delivering a customer's order in smaller batches over a period of weeks may not be costly to you, but this could be hugely valuable to a customer who has very limited storage space.

▷ If you're a large, cash-rich organization, offering a customer 30-day payment terms instead of asking for payment on delivery may be of little consequence to you, but this could be hugely beneficial to a customer who needs cash to fund their other needs.

Of course, the same principles can apply in reverse.

▷ It costs little for a customer to agree that you can use their story as a case study to help influence and persuade other prospects, or to introduce you to a prospective customer that they know well. But both of these actions could give a significant boost to your sales performance.

▷ Similarly, a customer might be happy to catch-up with you via phone or video call on alternate months, instead of you visiting their premises every time. The time taken up by these monthly conversations may be no different for them, but the reduction in travel time might be hugely valuable to you if they're a customer who's significantly isolated or far away from your home location.

So when discussing how you could change the shape of the deal, try to focus on two things:

1. adding or focusing attention on variables that are of high value to them, but are low cost for you; and

2. removing, or avoiding adding, any variables that are of low value to them, but are a high cost for you.

Negotiation golden rules

Here are four *do's* and four *don'ts* for effective negotiations.

1. ***Don't* make the first offer if you can avoid it.** By the time you get to a negotiation in a New 7-Step Sales conversation, you've already made the first offer; you made your offer when you presented your initial recommendation. That's why, if a customer isn't happy with what you've proposed and presented, it should be up to *them* to tell you what they want to change about the deal, and by how much.

   However, most people are reluctant to make the first move in case they either under compromise – leading to the other party becoming disheartened and disengaged, or in case they over compromise and concede more than they need to. So if you do have to make the first offer or concession in order to keep the deal moving, remember: (a) your initial proposal was a win-win – so you shouldn't need to move by much; and (b) if you're going to move, so must they; don't offer any concession without asking for something in return.

2. ***Don't* accept their first offer.** Conventional negotiation wisdom says you should always start by 'pitching high', which is why most customers will open a negotiation by demanding something that's more than they'd be happy to accept if challenged. This is why you shouldn't usually accept a customer's first counteroffer. If you *are* tempted to do so, you should only accept it if: (a) you

think it's fair; and (b) you establish that your customer is happy to close the deal without asking for further concessions if you do.

3. **Propose, but *don't* try to close (yet).** Negotiating is the process of reaching agreement on a shared goal through compromise by discussion. So just like you did earlier in your sales conversation, you will make proposals during your negotiation. However, a negotiation is best treated as a collaborative activity, so take a slightly softer approach by making proposals using words such as '*What if we…*', rather than words like '*I recommend…*', as the latter may feel like you're trying to take control and close off other options.

    Approaching things this way helps to demonstrate that although you still have confidence in your original proposal, you are open to other suggestions and are keen to find a way forward.

4. ***Don't* give anything away for free.** If they ask, then you reply, '*If you… – then I…*'. These are the four most important words in a negotiation. These words or, more accurately, the trading principle that sits behind them, are sometimes all that's needed to prompt a customer to back down if they make a 'cheeky' (or even downright rude) request for you to compromise. Just knowing that if they ask for something you're going to want something in return will encourage them to think carefully about what they request and how they request it – and it will stop you looking like a pushover.

So those are the four *don'ts* of a negotiation. Here are the four *do's*.

5. ***Do* watch out for the 'salami effect'.** This is when you trade away more than you planned for, one small slice at a time. Once your customer feels you've conceded to their demands in one area, they may become more inclined to ask for further concessions in others – just to see how much they can get away with. This is why its important to isolate all of your customer's issues or objections *before* you start to negotiate, and then, when you open your negotiation, you work through them one by one.

    Not only will this help to give your negotiation conversation structure, and a sense of progression, but following a list your customer created, prioritized and agreed was finite, will discourage them from asking for more and more, one slice at a time. This is especially true if you deal with each issue on the list in isolation, and ensure you gain agreement on the solution to that *before* you move onto the next area for discussion.

6. ***Do* keep your bottom line to yourself.** While it's OK to discuss the fact that you *have* limits, there are a number of reasons why you shouldn't reveal what they are.

When salespeople say their bottom line is that they couldn't accept less than X, most *would* be willing to accept less than X in the right circumstances. The same is true for customers. When a customer says their bottom line is that they won't pay a penny more than Y, most would be willing to do that if the other elements of the deal were right. People know this, which is why, in a negotiation when someone appears to openly reveal their bottom line, their counterpart usually doesn't (and probably shouldn't), believe it to be true.

If you were to share what your bottom line is, you'd potentially create two problems for yourself: (a) that's now what the customer will expect – after all you've just told them that while you could be happier, your bottom line would still be acceptable; and (b) even if you shared your bottom line believing it to be true, something about the deal could change that would make you revaluate your position – which would just make you appear dishonest. Neither is good, which is why you should always keep your bottom line to yourself.

7. ***Do* pause, and use silence to your advantage.** When in conversation, most people find protracted periods of silence uncomfortable. When this happens during a negotiation, people typically: (a) talk to break the silence and ease their discomfort – which often leads to them revealing information they would have been better off withholding; or (b) take the silence to be an indicator that the other person is unhappy with their last comment or proposal – so they back down without the other party having to say a word.

You can use silence to your advantage by deliberately pausing in certain situations. For example, if your customer rejects a proposal you've just made without making a counteroffer, don't immediately respond with a lower offer. Pausing before you respond, perhaps for five or six seconds, might be all that's needed to get them to rethink their position. If they don't, then your pause helps to show that you're not desperate, that you feel your proposal is fair, and that you have little room or incentive to move by much.

Pausing can also be an effective tactic in other situations too. For example, if your customer makes what you consider to be a generous offer, perhaps one that you feel you'd be foolish to turn down by pushing for more, at the very least you should pause before accepting it. This can reduce the risk that your customer will recognize they've been overly generous, and reduce any chance they'll suffer from buyer's remorse later.

8. *Do take your time.* As the previous point illustrates, taking time to think in a negotiation is no bad thing, especially if you stay silent while you do so. However, taking your time becomes especially important when the pace of the negotiation changes, particularly when the other party suddenly changes their position, or jumps on an offer you've just made and moves quickly to try to close the deal.

   When this happens, a good tactic is to run through the deal with your counterpart point by point, clarifying that your understanding matches theirs *before* you agree to the deal. Doing so will not only help to ensure that you're both on the same page, but it will also give you time to focus on what you're about to agree, to ensure you haven't missed something.

What's next?

Hopefully your negotiation has enabled you to co-create a compromised solution that you're both happy with. A great way to verify that is to summarize the new deal, then drop back to ask the customer another trial close question, such as 'How does that sound now?'

But even if you haven't been able to negotiate a way forward, you *are* going to have to bring the conversation to a close. Either way, your next step is going to involve closing in one shape or another, so that's where we're headed now.

Step 6
Close the sale

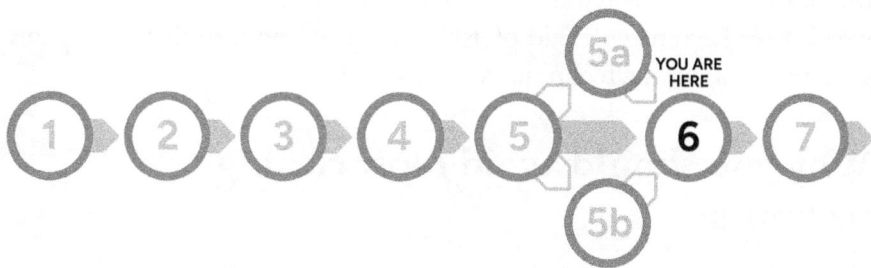

Figure 21: The New 7-Step Sale – Step 6

Why *you* need to close the sale

In sales, *closing* is defined as the point where the prospect conveys their positive buying decision to the salesperson. It's the point when your customer confirms they're happy to buy, or buy-into, your recommended solution.

> *Closing a sale means gaining a customer's clear and*
> *unambiguous agreement to your proposal.*

Unfortunately, most customers are unlikely to close the sale themselves. It's like being in a restaurant. Some customers are reluctant to call the waiter over even though they're ready to order, and would rather wait until they're asked. Other customers find it so difficult to make a decision, they need the encouragement of the waiter asking the question before they'll finally commit to what they want. Some people *are* comfortable enough both to call the waiter over *and* state what they want, but even those people often have a better experience if the waiter plays an active role, and are probably more likely to order appetizers, sides and dessert if asked.

So just like the waiter, you need to ask the question. But you also need to ask at the right time. Too early, and the customer may not yet be ready. But wait too long, and customers who are ready to buy may get frustrated at what they perceive is becoming a long-winded process; or, worse still, they'll just wander off to buy elsewhere.

Despite knowing this, many salespeople still find closing the sale to be a daunting task. Fear of rejection creeps in, and they find themselves going round in circles as they wait for the customer to close for them. Or, much worse, they become so afraid of asking a direct question that they resort to less ethical closing techniques.

Why you should avoid most closing techniques

We've defined that closing the sale means gaining your customer's clear and unambiguous agreement to your proposal. In Chapter 1, we also defined that ethical selling involves helping people to make informed buying decisions by exploring and targeting win-win outcomes, while being honest, truthful, influential and persuasive, but never manipulative.

Testing a closing technique against those definitions can help you to determine whether it's likely to be both ethical and effective.

Unfortunately, if you examine many popular closing techniques in detail (and feel free to Google some to check for yourself), you'll find that most don't pass that test. Here are some of the common faults.

> ▶ **Fault 1: It's not a definitive closing technique.** Some closing techniques might prepare a customer to make and share their buying decision, or draw out an indication that they're probably ready to do so, but they stop short of asking for the customer's clear and unambiguous agreement. This is why the trial close I

presented earlier isn't a *definitive* closing technique; it's simply one step in the process that leads you towards the *separate* step of closing the sale.

If a technique relies on a question that doesn't ask the prospect for their clear, unambiguous and definitive agreement to the solution you've presented, or worse still, doesn't involve asking a question at all, then it's not a definitive closing technique, and you shouldn't rely on it to close a sale.

▶ **Fault 2: It's a wholly assumptive technique.** Some popular closing techniques are designed to railroad the customer into moving forward based on the assumption that the customer's answer is 'Yes', despite never actually gaining their clear and unambiguous agreement. Here are some examples of some wholly assumptive closing questions:

'How would you like to pay?'

'How many shall I put you down for?'

'Which type would you like to buy?'

At best, wholly assumptive closes like these are misguided. The salesperson uses the closing technique believing that by doing so they've gained their customers agreement – as long as the customer doesn't object and goes along with what they're being 'encouraged' to do – then everything's OK. But ignorance is no defence. Using wholly assumptive questions to close a sale is both manipulative and unethical, and you need to avoid them at all costs.

▶ **Fault 3: It's a technique designed to trigger an 'automatic' response.** As you know from Chapter 4, we all rely on mental short-cuts to help us make quick and easy decisions without having to expend significant mental effort. For example, when we recognize something's becoming increasingly scarce that typically makes us want it even more, and we feel compelled to make a quick decision to buy it – driven by our fear of missing out. That's why limited time offers usually help to drive sales.

When used honestly and truthfully within the preceding steps of the sales conversation, *weapons of influence* like these can be used both ethically and effectively. However, if they're introduced or heavily referenced as part of closing a sale, some customers will see them as examples of trickery and manipulation. When you're closing a sale, you need to avoid any technique that's specifically designed to trigger such automatic responses.

So if those are some examples of what *not* to do, what *should* you do instead?

The best way to close a sale

The most ethical and effective way to get your customer's agreement, is to ask a simple and direct closed-ended question – one that seeks a simple 'yes' or 'no' answer.

For example, 'Would you like to go ahead?' or
'Shall I get that ordered for you?'

Of course, how you ask the question is still important. You need to be careful not to use leading or manipulative language, because you don't want to trigger any last-minute reactance if your customer believes you're trying to push them into saying 'yes'. But it's still important to ask the question with confidence, to show that while you assume their answer is going to be 'yes', as a professional and ethical salesperson, you're going to ask anyway.

This is important, because if the customer senses any hesitation or indecision on your part, that's likely to affect their decision. After all, if you've positioned yourself as an expert consultant and trusted advisor, if you're not confident about moving forward, then why should they be?

If you explored their needs correctly during the understanding step, recommended a way forward by delivering a personalized presentation, used your trial close and helped the customer to overcome any objections they might have, and hopefully saw some buying signals along the way, then at this point you *should* be confident. But even if you've followed the process and you're still not overly optimistic, then you've got nothing to lose by asking the question anyway. You need to bring the conversation to a close, so even if the answer is a 'no', you can at least then move on to invest your time and energy elsewhere.

*You need to ask for the sale. It's good to be confident and
assumptive when you do, but you must still ask.*

What to do if you don't get a 'yes'

How to handle persistent objections

What happens if you followed all of the preceding steps correctly, and
then asked a simple and direct closing question, only to receive a response
like: *'Leave it with me as I need to run this by my boss. I'm speaking with her on
Monday, so come back to me after that and I'll have a decision for you.'*

In situations like this you have three options.

- ▷ **Option 1:** Attempt to handle and overcome their objection so
  you can continue.

- ▷ **Option 2:** Revert to a fall-back objective.

- ▷ **Option 3:** Walk away.

If that was the first time you heard that objection from the customer, then
of course you should definitely choose Option 1 and attempt to handle
and overcome their objection. But what if you walk the customer through
your AEIO objection-handling process, only to be handed the exact same
objection again? This is where Option 2 comes in, and you should revert
to a fall-back objective.

While a fall-back objective wouldn't involve you making a sale today,
achieving one should move your customer one step closer to their buying
decision, and increase your chances of successfully closing the sale next
time. So now's the time to fall back on an objective like that, which, in
the previous example, would probably be to set a time for you and your
customer to speak, once they've spoken with their boss.

But if you think back to 'Step 1: Plan and prepare', you should recall that
every conversation-specific objective must require some form of active
commitment from the customer. So in this case, you'd only achieve your
fall-back objective if the customer agrees when, where and how you're going
to speak, and ideally blocks that time out in their diary. A vague agreement
along the lines of, 'OK, let's talk on Tuesday' wouldn't be enough.

In this example, Option 3, to walk-away, doesn't make sense, as there still seems to be a reasonable chance you could close this sale in future. But there are times when walking away *is* the right thing to do.

How to handle rejections (or insurmountable objections)

No matter how good your objection handling skills are, there will always be some objections you can't get past. Sometimes you'll deal with customers where the gap between your two positions is so large, no amount of persuasive objection-handling or deal-changing negotiation is going to bridge it. You either can't meet their immovable demands, or you'd put yourself in a losing situation by doing so.

When an objection is truly insurmountable, it becomes a rejection. Rejections are inevitable, but rather than just chalk them up to experience, there are two things you need to do when you receive one.

1. **Sincerely thank the customer.** Just because your product or service isn't right for the customer *now*, that doesn't mean they won't necessarily come back to you at a later date if their situation changes. And just because your solution isn't right for *this* customer, that doesn't mean they won't recommend it to someone else if they think it might be right for them. However, they're not going to do either if you part ways on a sour note. It's not their fault your solution isn't right for them, nor is it necessarily yours. So make sure you thank them for the time and energy they've invested into exploring the situation with you.

2. **Carry it forward as a learning experience.** There is always something you can do to improve, and the way to accelerate that process is to ensure you embrace your growth mindset and take steps to try to learn from every experience. We'll look at how to do that as part of the 'follow-up' step in the next chapter.

What to do when it's just not working

Sometimes it can be difficult to know at what point you should accept defeat. For example, what if you repeatedly don't get the 'yes' you're hoping for, but don't get a clear 'no' from the customer either? Or what if, despite your best efforts, you're continually faced with objections or brush-offs from a customer who seems adamant on derailing your sales conversation?

Knowing when to call it a day and walk away can be difficult, but your decision to do this should be based on three key factors.

1. **The size of prize.** How big is the gap between the customer's existing value to you (which could be nil if they're simply a prospect at this stage), and the potential value you could gain from the sale? The bigger the potential return, then the more investment it's usually worth making. Often, it's persistent salespeople (but not the pushy ones), who are most successful in the long run.

2. **The strength of your relationship and it's direction of travel.** As part of the planning and preparation step, we explored that the strength of your relationship with the customer is a useful metric to help gauge whether you're likely to win the prize that's on the table. Typically, the better the strength of your relationship, and the bigger the size of prize, the more persistent it's worth you being.

   The one caveat is that if you're selling to an existing customer and attempting to grow the size of their account, then not only is the strength of your relationship important, but so is its direction of travel. If the strength of your relationship is declining as a direct result of your attempts to get them to buy more, this is a sign that: (a) something about your approach is wrong – perhaps you're being too pushy; or (b) it's time to accept defeat with this particular sale, and focus on retaining and protecting their existing level of business while you consider whether a different approach would be better.

3. **The nature of the brush-offs or objections you're receiving.** Don't be afraid or perturbed by repeated non-specific brush-offs. If the size of prize, the strength of your relationship and its direction of travel are all good – keep going. With a little more persistence and effort, sometimes situations that seemed hopeless can become a glorious success.

   But if you're getting the same specific objections over and over, you're handling them in the right way, and have tried a number of different techniques to help the customer overcome them, all to no avail, then it might be time to accept defeat in relation to that particular objective.

If you do decide to accept defeat, remember to thank the customer for their time, and don't just walk away and forget about it. Reflect on what you can learn from the experience that might help you to become more successful in future, and set a reminder to revisit the customer at a later date when their situation, or yours, might have changed.

What's next?

Regardless of whether you successfully closed the sale, or just respectfully brought the sales conversation to a close, the process doesn't end there – you always need to follow-up. So let's move on to the final step of the New 7-Step Sale and look at how to do that.

Step 7
Follow-up

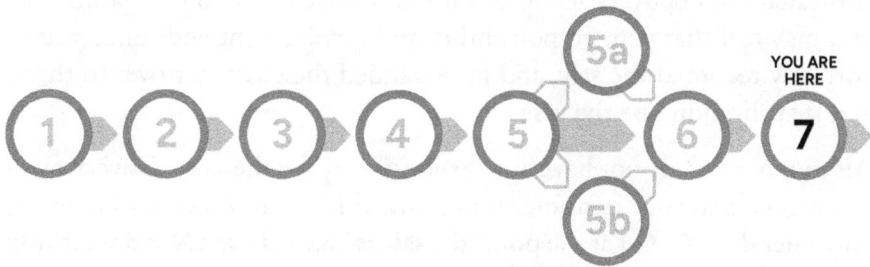

Figure 22: The New 7-Step Sale – Step 7

Your objectives for the follow-up step are:

1. deliver the sale you closed;

2. monitor your customer's satisfaction; and

3. drive continual improvement.

While the first and second objectives only apply if you successfully closed the sale, the third objective – driving continual improvement – is always important regardless.

As part of the follow-up step you'll also need to complete any post-conversation admin set by your organization, such as logging the conversation – and potentially the sale – in your CRM system. While I obviously can't know exactly what those tasks are for you, the purpose behind many of them will be to support or drive one or more of those objectives.

Let's look at what achieving each of those objectives involves.

Objective 1: Deliver the sale

'Sales delivery' refers to the process of providing a customer with the product or service that was sold, and fulfilling the promises that were made to them during the sales conversation. It encompasses the customer experience from the point they say 'yes' – and agree to buy, through to the point when they receive access to the product or service they bought and start to use it.

In most organizations, delivering the sale is not the sole responsibility of the salesperson – it typically involves teamwork. Some companies have a dedicated sales delivery team, and if that's the case in your organization, you may feel that your responsibility and involvement ends once you've correctly recorded the sale, and have handed the customer over to them. But that shouldn't be the case.

Although you may not have any responsibility for the sales delivery team or process (and your customer may know this), your responsibility to the customer doesn't end at the point the sale is handed over. Nor does it stop completely – even once a customer is in receipt of what they bought – because, if anything goes wrong at any point in the delivery process, or if the customer gets buyer's remorse shortly afterwards, they're still likely to blame you, at least in part.

Quite simply, whether it's part of your role or not, you need to follow the sales delivery through, because you can gain a lot from ensuring your customers are, and remain, happy.

Objective 2: Monitor your customer's satisfaction

Why is customer satisfaction so important?

It's no secret that creating happy customers is the key to building and growing a successful business. But it's important to recognize that happy customers (and unhappy ones) can directly impact *your* personal sales performance too. Here are some statistics to demonstrate why customer satisfaction should be something you care deeply about.

- According to research conducted by ThinkJar, 72% of customers will share a positive experience with six or more people. So happy customers can help you to win new customers, and if you know who they are, you can increase their impact by proactively sharing their story with other prospects and customers too.

- According to the global accounting firm PWC, 86% of buyers are willing to pay more for a great customer experience. So providing a great sales experience can encourage your customers to buy from you, even if your competitors are cheaper.

- A customer experience impact report published by Emplifi shows that 86% of consumers who quit doing business with a company do so because of a negative customer experience. So an unhappy customer is unlikely to remain an active customer for long.

- ThinkJar research also shows that, on average, only 1 in 26 unhappy customers actually complain; the rest just leave. So unless you actively listen, or proactively ask for feedback, you're unlikely to hear about your customer's problems until it's too late.

- According to Lee Resources International, when customers leave because they're actively dissatisfied, there's a 91% chance they won't do business with that company again. So you're unlikely to be able to win back a customer who actively stopped buying from you because they were unhappy.

- Statistics published by the Office of Consumer Affairs show that dissatisfied customers typically tell between 9 and 15 other people about their experience; while some tell 20 or more. So unhappy customers will not only leave, they'll also make it harder for you to win new business from other customers to replace what you've lost.

While the numbers in these statistics will undoubtedly vary from sector to sector, and from business to business, the principles behind them are sound. So monitoring and reacting to your customer's satisfaction is something you need to do.

How to monitor customer satisfaction

While there are many strategies companies can use to gather customer feedback, if your organization doesn't have a strategy in place, then as a frontline salesperson it's probably outside of your remit to implement one. Either way, that doesn't mean you can't gather feedback from the customers you work with. Here are three ways you can do that.

1. **Reflect back on your sales conversations.** Even if your sales conversations aren't recorded, that doesn't mean you can't review and reflect on them afterwards. Objections are one way that customers may actively share feedback during sales conversations. But even if you didn't receive any explicit feedback, you can still gain useful insights by listening actively. By paying attention to the language your customers use during your sales conversations (both verbally and non-verbally), and within any after-sales communications, you can often gauge how a customer is feeling.

2. **Ask your customers.** You can do this yourself, although if you're asking for feedback on the sales experience you provided personally, some customers may be reluctant to give you negative feedback directly. So one alternative is to have a colleague contact a few customers, to conduct a short customer satisfaction call. This could take the form of an interview, or it could be a much less formal conversation based around just one or two questions, as in the example I'll provide shortly.

3. **Conduct a mini survey.** Surveys are great ways of gathering customer feedback. Online surveys are especially useful, as the process can be largely automated, and many customers will feel more comfortable providing feedback over what can be an anonymous channel. However, these surveys don't have to be long or complicated in order to be effective. In fact, you can gather useful customer feedback by asking one simple question such as:

   Based on your sales conversation, rate how likely you are to recommend our company to a relevant friend or colleague, on a scale from 0 – for 'very unlikely' – to 10 – for 'very likely'.

   This question comes from the Net Promoter System®, developed by Bain and Company. When the answers from lots of customers are collated, the results can be used to calculate the organization's Net Promoter Score[SM]. However, you can also use individual customer scores to help create your prioritized action plan – as I described in 'Step 1: Plan and prepare'. You can also input them into the Greater Sales Planning Tool, which you can download for free by going to greatersales.com/bookextras.

Objective 3: Drive continual improvement

As we explored in Chapter 6, by harnessing the power of marginal gains, not only can you get a little better every time, but when applied consistently, this approach can significantly improve your sales performance.

This important principle explains why, in the New 7-Step Sale diagram (see Figure 8), there's an arrow leading back from the follow-up step to the first step of planning and preparation, closing the loop. This is because you can use what you learn from each customer interaction, to help you plan and prepare more effectively for the next.

Gathering customer feedback can be an important part of this process, but only if you do something with it. If your customer feedback isn't helping you or your organization to improve, you should either change what you collect *or* how you use it, so it does. Or, you should stop collecting it at all.

This is especially true for customer feedback you collect proactively. If you go to the trouble of asking your customers for their feedback, and then don't act on it, that's worse, and potentially more damaging than not asking for it in the first place. Rather than the customer just feeling their concerns aren't being heard, if you take the time to listen but don't respond and act on their feedback, they'll feel like they're being actively ignored.

But you don't have to rely on what your customers are saying; you can also drive continual improvement by reflecting on what you experienced too, and use that to decide what your next marginal gain should be. Here's how to do that.

What? So what? Now what?

Every day's a school day, and every sales conversation is an opportunity for you to learn and improve – regardless of whether you successfully closed the sale or not. If you did successfully close the sale, you might be able to learn from reflecting on why that happened. Was there something different about this customer, or how you approached each step of the sale, that you could apply to future sales conversations? Or could this be a case study you could share with other customers as a 'feel, felt, found' story?

Of course the same is true if you weren't able to get the sale across the line. What were the barriers to you being able to do that? What can you learn that might help you to avoid, or overcome, similar obstacles in future?

The 'What? So what? Now what?' technique I'm about to show you, is a powerful way to drive this type of reflective learning. It's a process for reflecting on sales conversations that can help you to identify even small opportunities to improve your sales performance.

It involves asking yourself three types of question, starting with '**What…?**' questions: What were the key aspects of your sales conversation that stood out for you? What did you do differently? What, if anything, did you forget to do? What did the customer do that seemed important?

You can also ask yourself questions based on the mindset chapter titles from Part 1, such as: What did you do to explore and target a win-win outcome? What indicated that there was enough trust for what you proposed? What did you do to add value through every step of the conversation? And, what do you think their gut feeling was and why?

Then you need to ask yourself '**So what…?**' questions. So what happened as a result? Did what you've identified impact what you thought or did in the moment, or could it have impacted how the customer reacted or responded? If so, what could that mean?

And finally, you need to ask yourself '**Now what…?**' questions. Now what will you do differently based on what you've learnt, that could help to improve the next conversation you have with this customer, or the conversations you have, or plan to have, with others? Or to return to our mindset-based question, how can you get a little better next time?

Not only is this 'What…? So what…? Now what…?' process a powerful technique to help you identify personal marginal gains, it's also a technique sales leaders can use to drive strategic improvement too.

A strategic improvement example

Here's an example of how Drinkit used this technique to analyse their sales and after sales experience, to create actionable insights and improve their overall sales performance.

What have we found out? The number of first-time customers who fail to make a second purchase from us is increasing. Despite analysing what happened during their initial sales conversations, no trends have been identified that explain why this might be happening. However, after looking at when these customers made their first purchase, this rise in lapsed customers correlates with customers who first bought from us during our recent cut-price promotion.'

So what **might this mean?** This might indicate that customers who are motivated to start buying from us due to a temporary price reduction, are no longer motivated to continue buying once the promotion ends and the price goes back to normal. This is potentially very damaging as these promotions are loss leaders, and a positive return on investment is only generated if we retain their business, *and* gain subsequent orders.

Now what **are we going to do differently as a result, to improve our sales performance?** Here are four things we're going to do as a result of what we've learnt through this exercise.

1. We're going to proactively contact lapsed customers who only made purchases during periods of heavy discounting, and attempt to win them back by demonstrating our value without focusing on price. We'll do this by helping them to understand that the benefits our products deliver, coupled with the pre and post-sales support we provide, more than makes up for any perceived higher-level of investment.

2. Next time we run a heavily discounted price promotion, we won't lead with the short-term price-reduction in order to close new business. Instead, we'll encourage customers to buy by identifying ways that our products can meet their needs on a long-term basis – demonstrating value in other ways to ensure that the price promotion is only used as an 'extra convincer', or 'golden hello'. That way, when the price promotion ends, the customer won't lose the main reason they started to buy from us in the first place, and so should be more likely to continue buying from us in the future.

3. When a customer makes their first purchase with us on a price promotion, we'll increase the level of after-sales support we provide, and schedule swifter follow-up calls with them to walk them through their next order.

4. We'll also ensure this information reaches our marketing team, so that they can take this into account when designing future

promotions. We'll suggest that future promotions should provide a lower level of discount over an extended period (across a customer's first two or three orders for example), as that could help customers to get into the habit of buying from us before their discount ends.

Alternatively, we could provide additional value to new customers in different ways, by funding consumer promotions rather than temporary price cuts for example. This might allow us to be just as successful at winning new business, without creating a perceived price increase after this initial support finishes.

What's next?

Although that brings us to the end of the New 7-Step Sale and the end of Part 3, there are two more areas I want to briefly cover to help you build on what you've learned and maximize the value you get out of this book.

Bonus chapter:
Your AI advantage

I've taken a human-centric approach in this book, and have deliberately stayed away from focusing on third-party tools – but AI deserves a special mention.

As a reader of this book you already have an AI advantage, but it might not be what you think. As we're the first generation of salespeople with access to AI, we all have an advantage over those who came before us. But in a world where some people are trying to find ways for AI to sell *for* them, the mindsets, knowledge and skills I've covered in this book are going to become more important than ever. As AI continues to develop and becomes ever more pervasive, in the future it may only be real-time, person-to-person sales conversations that buyers really trust, or certainly that they value most highly.

So you potentially have two AI advantages, but only if you apply what you've learnt through this book *and* utilize your growth mindset to continually learn how to use new technologies, including AI, to augment your human-first sales conversations. I don't believe AI will ever replace you as a frontline salesperson. But I do believe there's a risk you'll get replaced by a frontline salesperson *who does use* AI, if you don't embrace it.

As I write, providers of sales CRM and sales enablement systems are busy embedding and improving the AI features within their platforms. Developers of generative AI systems such as OpenAI, Anthropic and Google, are also coming up with ever more imaginative ways that AI can help us with our day-to-day sales activities too.

So much so, that anything I write here has the potential to quickly become out of date. So for the latest view of how AI could help you to have greater sales conversations, go to greatersales.com/bookextras – as that's where you'll find resources that are easier for me to update as technology improves.

However, in case you're in the dark or even dismissive of just how much AI can do, here are some examples of how it can already help.

▶ **Understanding what you're selling.** AI tools can help you to research products and services; identify key features, advantages and potential benefits; and conduct comparative analysis.

▶ **Understanding who to target.** Generative AI can help you to research and understand your target market; develop your ideal customer profile; and investigate where you may have a competitive advantage. AI tools within CRM systems can also help to refine these processes further, by analysing your sales and customer interaction records.

▶ **Setting personal objectives and targets.** AI-generated dashboards within CRM systems can help you to set personalized sales objectives and targets based on live data, and can then help to measure your performance against them.

▶ **Sales pipeline management.** AI-enabled CRM systems can automatically update a customer's pipeline status based on conversation outcomes, and help you to identify prospects and customers who represent significant opportunities or risks.

▶ **Sales planning and preparation.** AI virtual assistants can help you to manage your diary; create prioritized customer contact lists; produce pre-call briefings summarizing customer histories; conduct customer research; and suggest possible conversation topics.

▶ **Customer engagement.** Generative AI can help you to create and refine personalized conversation starters that adhere to set rules, such as the Confident Engagement Framework shared earlier in this book. AI phone and video-call plugins can already monitor speech patterns and provide real-time feedback on speed, tone and engagement levels – it's probably only a matter of time before something similar is also available via wearable devices too.

▶ **Understanding customer needs and wants.** Generative AI can help you to create and refine your go-to bank of 'good questions to ask', and help you to personalize these for significant segments, prospects or customers. Conversational AI can also help you to practise asking and responding to questions in real time role-plays, where the AI plays the part of a customer based on a specific profile you've given it. AI can also provide feedback afterwards by providing a transcription of your conversation, then analysing your performance against a specific framework or set of objectives.

▶ **Creating, proposing and presenting solutions.** Generative AI can help to produce sales aids and interactive content that's personalized for a specific customer, or that helps to demonstrate a particular competitive advantage. AI tools within sales enablement platforms can even help to do this on the fly during interactive video calls.

▶ **Overcoming objections and negotiating.** AI can help you to consider things from the customers point of view to predict objections you might face, help you to explore how you might be able to prevent them from occurring, and help you to prepare and practise your response in case they are raised.

▶ **Closing sales.** If you follow the techniques I've laid out in this book you don't need AI's help here. In Step 6 I explained why *you* need to close the sale, and why you should avoid most closing techniques – those principles apply here too. So I recommend you steer clear of AI at this stage of your sales conversation, and rely on your intuition and on the human connection you've built with your customer.

▶ **Following up after sales.** If your sales conversation took place by phone or video, then AI can produce automated notes and follow-up actions for you. But regardless of how your conversation took place, AI can help you to craft personalized follow-up messages, and keep track of what you need to do next and when you need to do it.

▶ **Driving continual improvement.** The more information AI has access to about your sales actions and conversations, the more it can help you to identify areas for potential improvement.

The need for caution

There are already lots of ways that AI can help you as a frontline salesperson. The list will undoubtedly grow quickly, but it's already largely limited only by your imagination. But while AI is an incredibly useful tool, you've got to use it with caution and treat it as a helpful assistant rather than something that can do everything for you.

Here are some of the things you risk if you over-rely on AI.

- ▶ **Loss of human connection.** Overdependence on AI risks reducing the authenticity of your human-to-human interactions, undermining your ability to build and maintain trust and rapport.

- ▶ **Inaccurate recommendations.** Generative AI generates new information, or generates new formats for existing information that comes from sources that may or may not be trustworthy. So while it's improving, at times it can, and does, provide incorrect or incomplete data – so you *must* verify that what it's telling you is correct before you rely on it or share it with a customer.

- ▶ **Unintended bias.** Outputs from AI systems are only as good as the information that goes in to create them, which includes the instructions you give. So AI can unintentionally reinforce your biases as well as any that exist in other sources, and can also misunderstand or misrepresent information as it tries to give you the answer it believes you're looking for.

- ▶ **Reduced adaptability and skill degradation.** Relying too heavily on scripted AI guidance is likely to hinder your ability to react quickly and effectively in unpredictable situations. Over-dependence on AI could also degrade your intuitive and critical thinking skills over time too.

So use AI, but use it with caution, and use it to supplement and help build your knowledge and skills – not replace them.

Next steps: Building on what you've learnt

Before we part ways, I want to briefly return to three topics I introduced at the very start of this book.

The first is that because I want this book to cover everything you need to think, know and do to have greater sales conversations, I've packed it full of everything I wish I knew when I started my sales career, almost 30 years ago. As a result, although I hope you've already got a lot out of reading it, I'm confident there's even more value waiting for you. So treat *How To Sell* as the handbook I intend it to be. Rather than trying to make one big change, focus on making lots of small ones, and keep coming back to the book over time for further inspiration.

The second point I want to make is that while this book contains everything you *need* to think, know and do to have greater sales conversations, sales is a big subject, and so it can't contain everything I can teach you. Nor can it contain everything there is to learn. But the mindsets, knowledge and skills in this book are solid foundations onto which you can build. As well as the free resources you can access at greatersales.com/bookextras, there are lots of other places you can learn from too, including many great sales books, some of which you'll find listed in the bibliography. So stay curious, embrace your growth mindset, and keep on learning.

But the point I want to end on is that developing the right mindsets, knowledge and skills won't *automatically* lead to greater sales results. If you refer back to Figure 1 – the performance drivers pyramid – in the introduction, you'll see there's a layer that sits between these and the outcomes you're aiming for, and that's your behaviours. Your behaviours define what you do and how you do it – they're essentially your mindsets, knowledge and skills in action. So that's what you need to do now – you need to put what you've learnt into action.

The practical examples throughout this book will help you to do that. But due to its nature, this book, like all other books, is quite instructional, because without an opportunity for us to interact that's all I can do. A good trainer, mentor and coach can help you take your learning to the next level. If that's something you'd like me to help with, then please feel free to reach out via my website at greatersales.com.

That said, you don't necessarily *need* a trainer, mentor or coach in order to improve. So if you don't have access to one, here are my top tips to help you put what you've learnt into action.

1. **Start now.** You don't have to be great to get started, but you won't become great unless you start. So choose something you can do that will help you to have greater sales conversations, and start doing it today.

2. **Don't try to do everything at once.** You know the power of marginal gains – small steps are OK, as long as you keep making them. It's OK to dream big, but it's also OK to start small.

3. **Learn – Do – Review.** Recognize that improvement doesn't stop at 'doing' – and learning and development should be a cyclical process. Reflecting back on what you did, and what you can learn from that to improve further, is a simple yet powerful technique for driving continual improvement. Don't worry about being perfect first time, but if it's particularly important that you don't get something wrong in front of a customer, then consider adding a rehearsal step so that it becomes learn, *practise*, do, review.

4. **Talk and ask for help.** To paraphrase the Pulitzer prize-winning poet Carl Sandburg, everyone is smarter than anyone. No one person has all the answers, so make the most of your network and listen, share and learn from each other, and if you need it, ask for help. I'd love to be part of your network too and continue to help if I can, so please feel free to reach out and connect with me on LinkedIn.

About the author

For more than 25 years, Steve Radford has been helping frontline salespeople to master the art of selling so their customers love to buy. A leader in sales learning and development, Steve has founded award-winning businesses, managed teams ranging from tens to hundreds of salespeople, and helped some of the world's biggest FMCG brands to develop high-performing sales capabilities.

Steve has also played a key role in elevating professional sales standards. At the University of Derby he co-created one of the UK's first university-accredited sales programmes, and at the Association of Professional Sales, he spearheaded development of the UK Government-backed Sales Executive Apprenticeship – setting new benchmarks for professional sales training.

Steve is a Founding Fellow of the Institute for Sales Professionals, and founder of the Greater Sales Company, where his passion for sales learning and development continues.

Acknowledgements

I'd like to thank everyone who's supported me throughout my sales career. The list is far too long to include everyone here, and it's hard to single out individuals, but I'm particularly grateful for the inspiration, energy and words of wisdom I've received from working with Laura Holden, Lara Vanden-Eynden, Paul Weedon and Richard John.

I'd also like to thank all the people who helped me to shape and refine this book into what it's become. Especially to my beta readers: Natalie Radford, Paul Weedon, Andy Hough, Trevor Moss, Jeremy Chestnutt, Richard John, Mark Jones, Nick Johncox and Dan Mukherjee. And to Alison Jones and everyone at Practical Inspiration Publishing.

Finally, I want to give my deepest gratitude to the most precious people in my life: to Natalie – my rock; to Sam and Heidi – my best work; and to Mum for making it all possible. Thank you for your support so that I could finally write the book I've been banging on about for so long.

Bibliography

Actman, Irwin and Taylor, Dalmas A. *Social Penetration: Development of Interpersonal Relationships* (Holt, Rinehart and Winston, 1973)

Baer, Jay. *Hug Your Haters: How to Embrace Complaints and Keep Your Customers* (Penguin Random House, 2016)

Barrick, Murray R., Mount, Michael K. and Judge, Timothy A. Personality and performance at the beginning of the new millennium (*International Journal of Selection and Assessment*, 2008)

Blount, Jeb. *Fanatical Prospecting: The Ultimate Guide to Opening Sales Conversations and Filling the Pipeline by Leveraging Social Selling, Telephone, E-Mail, Text and Cold Calling* (Wiley, 2015)

Blount, Jeb and Iannarino, Anthony. *The AI Edge: Sales Strategies for Unleashing the Power of AI to Save Time, Sell More, and Crush the Competition* (Wiley, 2024)

Cialdini, Robert. *Influence: The Psychology of Persuasion*, Revised Edition (HarperCollins, 2007)

Cialdini, Robert. *Pre-Suasion: A Revolutionary Way to Influence and Persuade* (Random House Books, 2016)

Covey, Stephen R. *The Seven Habits of Highly Effective People*, revised and updated (Simon and Schuster, 2020; page 248)

Dixon, Matthew and Adamson, Brent. *The Challenger Sale* (Penguin Publishing Group, 2011)

Dubinsky, A. J. A factor analytic study of the personal selling process (*Journal of Personal Selling & Sales Management*, 1981)

Earle McLeod, Lisa. *Selling with Noble Purpose: How to Drive Revenue and Do Work That Makes You Proud*, 2nd Edition (Wiley, 2020)

Fox Cabane, Olivia. *The Charisma Myth: How to Engage, Influence and Motivate People* (Penguin Group, 2012)

How to Increase Your Sales, Training manual (The System Company, 1920)

Kahneman, Daniel. *Thinking, Fast and Slow* (Farrar, Straus and Giroux, 2012)

Kano, Noriaki, et al. Attractive quality and must-be quality (*Journal of the Japanese Society for Quality Control*, 1984)

Keenan, Jim. *Gap Selling: Getting the Customer to Yes* (A Sales Guy Publishing, 2018)

Kross, E., Berman, M. G., Mischel, W., Smith E. E. and Wager T. D. Social rejection shares somatosensory representations with physical pain (The Proceedings of the National Academy of Sciences, 2011)

Kruger, F. (ed.) *The Neurobiology of Trust* (Cambridge University Press, 2021)

McDonald, Malcolm. *Market Segmentation: How to Do It and How to Profit from It*, Revised 4th Edition (Wiley, 2012)

Peale, Norman V. *The Power of Positive Thinking* (Vermillion, 2004)

Pink, Daniel H. *Drive: The Surprising Truth About What Motivates Us* (Canongate Books, 2018)

Rackham, Neil. *SPIN Selling: Situation, Problem, Implication, Need-Payoff* (McGraw-Hill, 1988)

Ross, Lee and Ward, Andrew. *Naive Realism: Implications for Social Conflict and Misunderstanding* (Stanford University Centre on International Conflict and Negotiation, 1995)

Schwartz, Barry. *The Paradox of Choice: Why More is Less* (HarperCollins, 2004)

Tamm, James W. *Radical Collaboration*, 2nd Edition: Five Essential Skills to Overcome Defensiveness and Build Successful Relationships (Harper Business, 2020)

Voss, Chris. *Never Split the Difference: Negotiating as if Your Life Depended on It* (Penguin Books, 2016)

Willis, J. and Todorov, A. First impressions: Making up your mind after a 100-MS exposure to a face (*Psychological Science*, 2006)

Zak, Paul J. The neuroscience of trust (*Harvard Business Review*, 2017)

Ziglar, Zig. *Zig Ziglar's Secrets of Closing the Sale* (Berkley Books, 1982)

Index

Please note that numbers are indexed as though spelled out: for example, 7 is indexed as seven. Numbers in *italics* indicate illustrations, figures or tables.

A quick word from Practical Inspiration Publishing...

We hope you found this book both practical and inspiring – that's what we aim for with every book we publish.

We publish titles on topics ranging from leadership, entrepreneurship, HR and marketing to self-development and wellbeing.

Find details of all our books at: www.practicalinspiration.com

Did you know...

We can offer discounts on bulk sales of all our titles – ideal if you want to use them for training purposes, corporate giveaways or simply because you feel these ideas deserve to be shared with your network.

We can even produce bespoke versions of our books, for example with your organization's logo and/or a tailored foreword.

To discuss further, contact us on info@practicalinspiration.com.

Got an idea for a business book?

We may be able to help. Find out about more about publishing in partnership with us at: bit.ly/PIpublishing.

Follow us on social media...

@PIPTalking

@pip_talking

@practicalinspiration

@piptalking

Practical Inspiration Publishing

www.ingramcontent.com/pod-product-compliance
Lightning Source LLC
Chambersburg PA
CBHW021923190326
41519CB00009B/889